# Fraternal Youth

## FATHERHOOD FAILS AND OTHER TALES
## WITH BOY-GIRL TWINS

### DARBY JONES

# Fraternal Youth

FATHERHOOD FAILS AND OTHER TALES
WITH BOY-GIRL TWINS

DARBY JONES

# Contents

# 1

# Diapers and **Grit**

I changed my first diaper on Monday, August 27, 2007. The smell reminded me of fermented mothballs with a touch of failed dreams. I don't know where those subtle notes came from, but they were good reminders to use birth control.

Melina and I had just started getting serious, so this was our first major test. Her brother, Paul, was in Paris participating in a 1200 kilometer bicycle race, so we were babysitting his kids for an entire week.

We were told that little Nick knew how to go number two in his potty chair, but the convenience of taking a dump in a diaper whenever and wherever is the obvious choice.

The smug smile on his face looked like it was mocking the anguish in mine. It can't be true, coming from a two-year old, but it felt like a premeditated power play to balance the scales, like maybe I should think twice about my eat-your-broccoli-before-dessert warnings.

Nicholas (in his mind): "How do you like this time-out?"

Me: "I'm going to barf."

Nicholas: "Mwahahahahaaaaaa!"

I couldn't help but sneak a smile while writhing in revulsion.

Me (in my mind): On second thought, I'd like to have one or two of these things someday. Sophie and Nicholas are too stinkin' cute. That, however, is not going to stop me from destroying them in the next pillow fight. I'll be ready this time.

Four years and two fraternal things later … Yabba dabba **two**.

# 2

# Yabba Dabba **Two**

### How to make a dad cry

Aug. 23, 2011 | 2 years, 5 months old

Finn was crying, so I slipped into the bedroom and knelt by his side. I didn't say anything – just kissed his salty eyes and scratched his head. As I walked out, before the door shut, he said in a worn-out voice:

"I love you too, Daddy."

### A nice lie to live up to

Oct. 11, 2011 | 2 y, 7 mo

Eating dinner.

Me: "What do you want to be when you grow up?"

Finn: "I want to be a conductor – catch bad guys."

Me: "Interesting. Fiona?"

Fiona: "I want to be a dinosaur."

Me: "Very good. I told you our family came from a long line of unicorns, didn't I?

Fiona: "No!"

Me: "Yeah, look. I've got the scar from the horn right here on my forehead to prove it. See?"

Fiona: "Whoa!"

Me: "But I didn't eat my broccoli, so my horn fell off. Yours hasn't even started growing, so you better eat up."

Fionasaurus Rex

Darbodactyl Doo

## You Have to Cry

Nov 18, 2011 | 2 y, 8 mo

Finn and Fio got in big trouble at the grocery store. Finn dropped a can of tinned-pork on Melina's middle toe. The SPAM survived, but Momma no longer has a piggy that eats roast beef. The toe's still there, but it's a scarred vegetarian now.

Next, Fiona stood up in the cart, which was totally unsanctioned. Melina was only looking away for a second, but of course, some helicopter mom had to swoop in and scold her.

Helicopter Mom: "Somebody needs to watch their daughter?"

Melina: "She's mine. [Under her breath] Sorry that I don't have eyes in the back of my head."

When they came home, I was judge, jury, and executioner. The plea bargain: If our little minions agreed to carry in the groceries, I'd reduce their sentence from five minutes to four. They asked for three, but considering the severity of the crime, I wouldn't budge – told 'em I'd throw in a pizza for dinner and they accepted.

So they carried the groceries in and proceeded to their time-out chairs. Fiona immediately started to cry, to which Finn (who had much more experience in time out) responded,

"Fiona, you don't have to cry in time out." Fiona stopped crying on a dime and shouted "B-bo! You HAVE to cry!"

I cocked my head back and roared with laughter, which put a stop to the argument … and the crying. Fiona accidentally chuckled.

"Gotcha!"

Caught her red-handed. I gotta hand it to her though. It was an Oscar-worthy performance.

Finn: "I hear what you're saying about the poo. I really do, but I still think the pee came first."

## Victory swagger

Dec. 23, 2011 | 2 y, 9 mo

Snowstorms delayed our Christmas flight to Raleigh and we were failing as parents. After an hour reading the same books, Fiona's restlessness turned to tantrum. The stares of people nearby started to look like bad words.

I tried to fashion a paperclip into a frog, but one bounce and it was gone. Then, the metaphorical light bulbs flashed as I got an idea. The "bulbs" were right there, staring me in the face in the form of three shiny silver helium balloons floating above the Christmas display by the gift store.

For the sake of everyone's sanity, I ran over and commandeered them for Fiona. As if I had flipped a switch, her crying turned to hysterical laughter. But the new crazy looked almost identical to the previous one and continued to attract glares. Clearly, her energy couldn't be contained in the small deli we were in, so I unleashed her to run the halls.

She wove through holiday crowds at top speed, balloons bobbing behind and occasionally grazing the faces of speed walkers. Before long, people were pointing and smiling.

I was thrilled to be back in society's good graces, but red alerts were still sounding in my head. Toddlers can't just run around willy nilly without something going horribly wrong. Sure enough, we all cringed as Fiona tripped over someone's luggage. Remarkably though, she had been hugging one of the balloons. Not only did it break her fall, but she slid a few feet across the tiled floor as she crash-landed.

I couldn't tell if the onlookers were getting up to see if she was okay or if they were giving her a standing ovation. In any case, Fio turned it into a game, running a bit faster this time and leaping into the air. A few of the power walkers leaped into the air themselves as she ran up behind them, sliding by like a belly-surfing penguin on ice.

TCA said to put everything in the box. I followed the rules, but X-ray dude looks grumpy for some reason.

It's too bad we didn't get in on camera. I would have captured the magic myself, except my hands were tied up doing traffic control. Passersby started clearing the way. Now the whole corridor was her personal runway ... until she leaped a little too high.

POW!

**Fiona hit the ground, still spread out like Superman as she slid to a stop. At this point, nobody seemed to care that the exploding balloon sounded like gunfire.**

TSA #1: "Yeaaaah, we're just going to let this one slide."

TSA #2: "You're fired."

TSA #1: "C'mon!"

TSA #2: "Ok, it was pretty good."

When Fiona stood up, the two other balloons pulled up and away. "Noooooo!" she cried. I jumped, but couldn't get there in time. That was it. The show was over. Fiona was bawling as I picked her up. As we walked back to the deli, I faintly heard someone behind me in the whiskey bar say, "Hey." I looked back and Dude was holding a chair. "I bet you can get her those balloons," he suggested.

I don't turn down a good dare, and this was close enough. The man was betting on me. Sure, Fiona played a part in it, but honestly, I wanted the audience to myself. The twins are always stealing the show.

I handed Fiona off to her mother to be consoled, but it was just a ploy to keep Melina distracted. She's a force to be reckoned with anytime, but especially when I show my ass.

So I grabbed the chair and quickly got to work, but my first attempt fell short. Dude looked disappointed, like my height was false advertisement. I was just another tall white guy with deceptively jumpy vibes.

I could see a few airport staff members pointing my way, trying to decide if I was going to be a problem. At least Melina wasn't watching. That meant there was still time to hatch a new plan. I spied a trash can that looked promising, but the thing was massive, made of stone – way too heavy to slide. What if …?

It took some muscle, but I was able to tip it over just enough to keep its contents from spilling out, but far enough to slowly roll it along the bottom edge.

It was part balancing, part Frogger as I wove through the speed walkers and grinned at all the what-the-fuck faces. As I climbed atop the big-ass trash can, onlookers from the deli, gift store and whiskey bar were all tuned in. That's when I saw my extremely bewildered wife cutting through the crowd. It was now or never.

[Alright Spielberg. I'll make it easy for ya'.]

```
FADE IN:
```

**INT. NASHVILLE AIRPORT – LARGE CORRIDOR – DAY**

```
The shrewd face of MELINA looks confused. The
warm face of BAR DUDE begins to smile, eyebrows
rise in anticipation. A walkie-talkie is heard
off-screen.
```

                    TSA #1 (V.O.)
                We've got a jumper. Repeat.
                We've got a jumper. Over.

IN SLOW MOTION - DARBY launches. Fingertips just
barely snag the end of the ribbon.

                                          CUT TO:

**EXT. SPACE**

GREEN SCREEN - DARBY'S hair is standing straight
up. We see stars, planets and a big fucking
supernova. We hear the string quartet crescendo.

                                          CUT TO:

**MEL'S POV**

Darby tucks and rolls, still clutching the
ribbon. Fiona jumps on him as the barflies
explode.

                                        FADE OUT

It would have been a Steven Spielberg ending had I not come down so
hard. Mel was the only one who could tell I was hurt, but I had so much
adrenaline pumping that my limp looked more like victory swagger.

As Fiona hugged my leg, I tied her fuzzy red glove to the ribbon and
tossed the two remaining balloons back up toward the ceiling. Her jaw
dropped in disbelief. Before she could get mad, the balloons started
to slowly drift back down with the weight of the glove. Fiona began
laughing, then clapping and stomping in anticipation.

When it was time for us to board, Fiona gave the balloons to a little
boy sitting on the floor. I almost lost it, watching him blush at my
little girl. I bet he kept that fuzzy glove.

As we floated back to Raleigh, Mel reminded me that I wasn't
Superman. Said I was pretty good at flying, but that I needed to work
on my landing. Fiona will have to teach me someday.

# 3

# **Three**nagers

## Twins that go bump in the night

Mar. 11, 2012 | 3 years exactly

Finn is really dragging family time out tonight.

Finn: "Can we get a net so we can hit the hockey ball into it?"

Me: "I'll think about it, but it's bedtime, so lights out."

Finn: "I'll dream about it. I only have one dream left. I'll tell you about it later."

Me: "OK, just don't get out of bed like you did last night. After bedtime, you play hockey in your dreams, not in the kitchen. You don't go body checking your sister into the walls or whatever the heck y'all were doing."

Finn: "But Daddy, I'm practicing."

Me: "For what?"

Finn: "To be a big boy."

Finn won that argument. It was a tactic I hadn't encountered before. He was too cute to fuss with. I made my point though, so if it happens again, I'll make my threenager an offer he can't refuse.

## Video: Carrots for Ra Ra (Rabbit)
April 8, 2012 | 3 y, 1 mo

"Carrots for Ra Ra"

## First memory
May 27, 2012 | 3 y, 2 mo

Me: "What did you dream about last night?"

Finn: "I was in a belly. Then I came out of the belly. And then I woke up."

Me: "Whoa!"

## Early fatherhood retirement
Sept. 7, 2012 | 3 y, 6 mo

Early morning. Melina's still asleep. Walking into the dining room.

Me: "Hey buddy, why are you sitting there?"

Finn: "Because Fiona cleaned up all the books and I didn't help."

I started laughing, so he cheered up.

Finn: "Can I get out now?"

Me: "Maybe. How long of a timeout did you put yourself in?"

Finn: "I don't know. I can only count to 100."

Me: "Did you learn your lesson?"

Finn: "Yes."

Me: "My job is complete. Let's play!"

## Taking a wee in your dream
Oct. 2, 2012 | 3 y, 7 mo

Dream journaling together on Finn's bed.

Me: "What would you like to dream about?"

Fiona: "I'm going to run over a chick."

Me: "That's your dream? Why do you want to run over a baby chicken?"

Fiona: "I don't. That's just what I'm going to dream about."

Me: "Stop laughing. I'm pretending your belly is a table and I can't write your dream down when you're giggling."

Fiona laughs harder.

Me: "Okay next. Finn, how 'bout you?"

Finn proceeds to tell me everything he can possibly think of.

Finn: "... and then I'm going to buy a new raccoon and transform into a lion."

Me: "Slow down!"

Finn: "And then I was a dragon and I saw some fairies fly over the water."

He takes a couple deep breaths and hops out of bed.

Finn: "This is a long dream, Daddy. And then I wake up and I get some juice and I have to go peepee!"

Me: "Incredible!"

Finn is dancing around.

Me: "Wait, you wanna take a pee in your dream?"

Finn's jumping up and down.

Finn: "No Daddy! I have to peepee right now but I can't reach the doorknob!"

Me: "Well it sounded like you were taking a wee in your dream."

Finn: "OPEN THE DOOR DADDY!!!"

## Selective hearing
Nov. 4, 2012 | 3 y, 8 mo

Finishing up dinner.

Me: "Hey Finn, didn't you say you'd drink your juice after dinner?"

Finn: "I didn't hear me say that."

Me: "Did you just say, 'I didn't hear me say that'?"

Finn: "Yes."

Me: "Well maybe you weren't listening to yourself. Drink your juice."

# 4

# **Four**nados

### There's a nice word for poop

Mar. 11, 2013 | 4 years exactly

Eating breakfast.

Me: "Happy Birthday! Do you like your birthday present?"

Fiona: "Daddy, I'm so happy we have a doggie!"

Me: "Awww, that makes me happy, baby."

Finn: "And I'm so happy you got the dog-doo off my shoe!"

Fiona and I laugh at this while Finn shouts over us.

Finn: "You don't call it poop! You call it dog-doo!"

Finn is so PC. A few days ago Fiona was hollering.

Fiona: "Wipe my butt, Daddy! I went poop!"

Finn: "Don't say 'poop,' Fiona. There's a nice word for poop."

Me: "What is it?"

Finn: "My raccoon told me."

Me: "Well, what's the word?"

Finn: "I don't know. I don't understand anything Raccoon says."

## Bugs 'n Spuds
Mar 20, 2013

Back in college, I remember two girls banging on my friend Sharon's apartment door while we were chilling out between classes. We thought it was an emergency, but come to find out, Girl#1 had merely trapped a big bug in the oven earlier in the day and needed help with disposal … but there's a catch. She was so satisfied with containing the cockroach, that she had gone about her day and forgot all about it. Later on, Girl#2 came home and whipped up a delicious batch of au gratin potatoes.

Of course, the cockroach did what I would have done in the same situation. Fifteen minutes later, the entire apartment smelled like a delicious batch of Grandma's Bugs 'n Spuds casserole. I can only hope that I'll be swimming in cheesy potatoes when I die.

Anyway, the girls assured me that if one of them dealt with it, they'd also be cleaning vomit out of the oven, which is where we came in. They knew their crazy neighbors would do anything for a buck.

Their pitch was short, but convincing. For five bucks, all I had to do was grab the taters, throw 'em in a bag, and chuck it out the window.

Me: "Done."

The girls were extremely thankful, except I could tell they didn't like that I took a bite first. But waste not, want not. That's what Grandma said. And Grandpa would lick the plate if nobody was looking. I saw him one time. All I'm saying is that sometimes you can slice a tiny bit of mold off and take a big juicey bite. Forget the fungi. It's mind over matter. Cut the yuck. Gobble the yum. In fact, "yum" should be a mantra we all meditate on a bit more in life.

"Yummmmmmmmmmmmmmmm."

I didn't know it at the time, but this experience was training grounds for my biggest gross out ever: Fatherhood.

## Where's the poop?
April 15, 2013

"Why does every room smell like poop?" I pondered. Maybe our new puppy, Piper, pottied inside again. So I searched all over, looking behind couches, under tables, but everywhere I went smelled equally foul.

"Meet Piper"

Me: "Sweety, I don't know how Piper did it, but the entire house reeks of dog-doo. Maybe she shat near one of the return air vents?"

Melina: "I don't smell anything Scooby."

"Wait a minute," I thought. "There's one other explanation." So I walked into the bathroom and it was just as I suspected.

**Me: [Hollering]: "Nevermind babe, it's just a piece of poop on my nose!"**

Melina: "What?!"

Me: "It's okay, your ears are working just fine."

Melina: "That's unfortunate."

Moments ago, I had just changed a messy diaper. Somehow a glob got on my finger and migrated north to my nose. There's always a logical explanation for shit like this.

Post contamination. Mel made me quarantine my nose.

## Tell me when I smell
June 1, 2013 | 4 y, 3 mo

Peaking into Finn and Fiona's room.

Me: "If you guys don't take a nap, we're not going to go to the dog park with Kenobi and Piper."

Fiona: "Daddy, we're not going to go to the dog park if you have stinky breath."

Me: "All the other dogs have stinky breath. Why can't I?"

Fiona: "Daddy, I have to tell you something. [whispering in my ear] You need to brush your teeth."

Me: "Thank you Fiona. I can always count on you to tell me when I smell. That's good. Finn just lets me stink. I'll brush my teeth if you take a nap. Deal?"

Fiona: "Deal."

Me: "Kiss?"

Fiona: "NO!"

## One twin loves me.
## One for two ain't bad.
Sept. 11, 2013 | 4 y, 6 mo

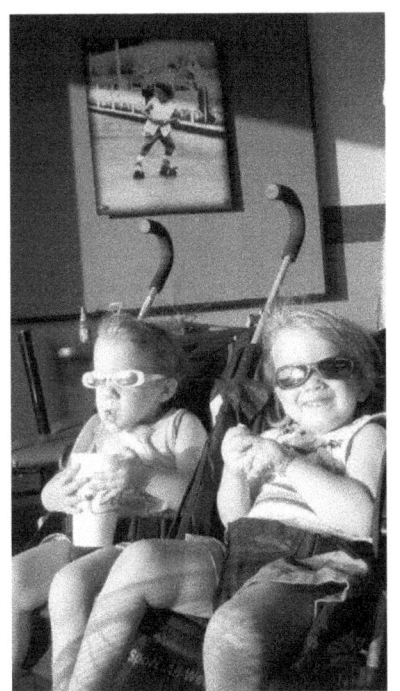

Getting home late from work. Everyone's already eating dessert.

Me: "I didn't get a mango creamsicle. Are there any left?"

Finn: "You can have a bite of mine." [Finn comes over and shares a bite.]

Me: [Looking at Fiona] "Thanks Finn!"

Fiona: "I was going to give you a bite, but it's in my belly now."

Me: "That's really thoughtful of you.

# Girls are smarter than boys

Dec. 9, 2013 | 4 y, 9 mo

Pulling out of the driveway. Late to school.

Me: "Thank you for putting your seat belts on all by yourselves. Y'all are good babies. But you're not really babies anymore, are you? It kinda makes me sad."

Finn: "Daddy, you can hold my baby."

Me: "You mean when you grow up?"

Finn: "Yeah, when I grow up and have a baby. You can even wipe its butt!"

Me: "Aww, thanks, Finn. That's so thoughtful."

Finn: "I'm going to tell Mrs. McKenzie when I get to school."

Fiona: "No, you can't do that. You'll get in trouble."

Me: "It's probably okay. But you should say 'bottom' instead of butt."

Fiona: "Girls are smarter."

Me: "Smarter than boys?"

Fiona: "Yeah."

Me: "Why is that?"

Fiona: "Because they're nice. They don't get in trouble. They tell the truth."

Finn: "That's not true."

## Shhhh!

Dec. 15, 2013 | 4 y, 10 mo

"Shhhh! … I heard a sound make a noise." – Fiona Frost

## The best Christmas ever

Dec. 18, 2013 | 4 y, 10 mo

Eating spaghetti.

Finn: "Daddy, you haven't given us your Christmas list. What do you want? Maybe some motorcycles or a bunch of beer or someone to snuggle up? Maybe some spicy spaghetti? I don't know. What do you want?"

Me: "All of that – what you just said. That pretty much sounds like the best Christmas ever!"

# 5

# Gimme **Five!**

### Videos: Fun with a hose

July 27, 2014 | 5y, 4 mo

I hope devices don't ruin summer.

"Fun with the hose (part 1)"

"Fun with the hose (part 2)"

## The big wind

Aug. 14, 2014 | 5 y, 5 mo

Finn and Fio crossed the street this morning while we were asleep. It was totally unsanctioned, but they had let Piper slip out the door and chased after her in hot pursuit. I couldn't believe Piper let them catch her, but there she was on the leash, in their hands.

Fiona: "We looked both ways, like five times."

Finn: "No six times! And then we were in Tom's yard, and there was this big wind, and Fiona said,

'LOOK!!!' and I looked, but there was nothing there. Then Fiona said, 'No. Look! Your pants fell off!' so I looked down and hahahahaha … she was right!"

Me: "Well no wonder you noticed the big wind."

## Music is power

Aug. 24, 2014 | 5 y, 5 mo

Eating lunch together.

Finn: "I don't know. Music is just ... boring."

This would have broken my heart, but I knew he was trying to get a rise out of me. Five years old and he already knows my soft spot.

Me: "Finn, music is the greatest thing in the world!"

Finn balks at my hyperbole.

Finn: "No, you and Mommy and Fiona are the greatest."

Me: "That's precious. Maybe I won't put you in timeout for such blasphemy."

Finn: "What's blas ...?"

Me: "Don't worry. I'm joking. But outside of the people you love, music is the best! Fiona knows what I'm talking about."

Fiona: "Yeah Finn. I love music."

Finn: "But do you like music more than treats?"

Clearly, he knows Fiona's weakness too. She has to think about it.

Fiona: "Yes ... when it's powerful."

Me: "YESSS! WHEN. IT'S. POWERFUL! Fiona you can have all the treats you want today!"

Fiona "Really?!"

Me: "Well, by 'treats' I mean watermelon and by 'all' I mean ... all. Sure. Have as much as you like, but after you finish your lunch."

## Chili dinner

Aug. 29, 2014 | 5 y, 5 mo

Finn: "What do you call a Finn who scarfs chili down?"

Me: "I don't know. What?"

Finn: "Scar Finn."

Me [laughing]: "It's your Irish mobster name! SCAR FINN!"

## Monday Morning Smackdown!

Sept. 10, 2014

Sitting at work. Bored out of my mind.

I didn't intend on going to Monday Morning Smackdown, but I suddenly found myself sitting front row in my cubicle. Out of nowhere, I heard a very adamant sounding "Caw! Ca-caw caw!"

I swiveled around to look out the window and witnessed two angry animals glaring at each other over a giant half-eaten Snickerdoodle.

The cookie was in the paws of Hank. Hank is also the name of a squirrel that I met in Memphis, so I've adopted the moniker for every squirrel I encounter. They're all the same. Hank's got balls of steel and a peanut for brains.

"Caw … Caw!" cried Crow as he backed Hank into the tree, threatening to claw the eyes out of Hank with each step. Escaping up the tree would require all fours, but Hank wasn't about to drop his cookie for no Crow. He held his ground, standing upright and eating furiously.

What he didn't cram down his face hole was stuffed into his cheeks. The crumbs stuck to his whiskers, further taunting Crow. Hank met every "Caw" with a demented cackle that sounded like Cartman gobbling an entire bag of Cheesy Poofs at once.

Every now and then Crow stopped and acted like he wasn't paying attention – pecking the ground and such, but Hank knew Crow had his periphs turned on. Suddenly Crow jumped, but Hank was cracked out on sugar, higher than Crow had ever flown, so he dodged the pounce faster than a preteen avoiding Dad's hug at a home game.

Enraged, Hank munched even faster and cackled even louder. This went on for a few minutes, until Crow stepped too close. Never dropping the cookie, Hank charged straight for Crow, hopping and shouting obscenities in squirrel speak.

Crow jumped up and hovered, wings kissing Hank's whiskers, before landing a respectful distance away as Hank finished the last morsel. Hank had a big fuck-you smile on his face as Crow bowed his head and flew off.

"This Sunday!!! Tune in to see returning welterweight champion Hank the NUT Cracker take on Chicken Chicka BOOOOM! Only on Pay-Per-View!"

## Special doctor

Nov. 7, 2014 | 5 y, 8 mo

I saw a special doctor recently. I wanted to talk to my mom about the situation, so I invited her over for dinner. When she asked about our day, Finn jumped right in.

Finn: "It was parent teacher conference day so we stayed home with Mommy. She took us to the park … and oh yeah, Daddy had to go to the butt doctor!"

Fiona: "Because he's not drinking enough water!"

I'm officially old. The butt doctor prescribed some cream for, as he put it, my "big-ass hemorrhoid!"

## Sick joke

Nov. 15, 2014 | 5 y, 9 mo

We've all been sick for the past few days, but I knew Finn was feeling better last night because he started to make up jokes.

Finn: "Why do our butts like each other so much?"

Me: "Hmmm, I don't know. Why?"

Finn: "Because we're butties."

## We have a problem here.

Nov. 29, 2014 | 5 y, 9 mo

The kids are finally splitting up, so we've been asking their opinions on new bedroom decor. While shopping at Walmart, I ask Finn if he wants us to buy this cool Star Wars piece.

Finn: "We have a problem here."

Me: "What is it?"

Finn: "Luke had the blue lightsaber, not Darth Vader. And Darth Vader should have the red one."

Me: "Wow. You look pretty serious. You sure?"

Mel [consulting Google]: "He's right."

Finn starts laughing. He looks so proud for knowing his pop culture and apparently the serious face is sarcasm. Cut to the checkout line at Walmart.

Me: "So my son pointed out that the light sabers here are actually the wrong color. We don't get a discount for that, do we?"

Cashier [glaring]: "... It's like, $5."

She doesn't catch my sarcasm. Maybe because I'm a frugal bastard and wasn't being sarcastic.

So Finn and Fiona have graduated. They're getting their own rooms. I don't tell them to go potty. They can go on their own. I really thought I'd rejoice when this day came, but honestly, I'll miss wiping butts. It's the beginning of them not needing me. I think I'll work on the song I started when they were itty-bitty. I need some nostalgia medicine.

This is all I've got so far.

> *Boogies in ya' NOSE! Crust in your EYE!*
> *Working on a POO makes you CRY.*
> *Cry for your supper. Cry for your sleep.*
> *You don't know numbers so you can't*
> *count SHEEP!*

"Finn & Fio's gag reel"

## Goosebumps

Jan. 2, 2015 | 5 y, 10 mo

The kids have a few options before going to bed (joke books, storytelling, dream-telling, etc.). Tonight we opted for massage. Finn likes to get one, but when we turn around, he doesn't return the love. Sure, he'll pound his fists. That's just fun, though.

So tonight I was surprised when he grabbed a cup of grass from his school project and started tickling my back. I've heard of this technique done in swanky spas, but I have to be honest: It's overrated. It sorta felt good until he tipped the over-watered grass sideways and dumped cold water down my pants. Also a technique I'd never experienced.

I was pretty upset until he convinced me that he didn't know it would happen. Finn and Fiona then had a good laugh. Finn said it reminded him of the day before when I had spilled juice all over myself. This cracked my grumpy face into a smile.

Fiona, on the other hand, is a great masseuse. And not just for her age. Her primary languages of love are touch, spending time, and helping out. She's not outspoken like Finn (which is why you don't see as many of her little quips), but she communicates in other ways. She churns her little fists, uses her elbows and feet. She likes walking on my back, which is amazing. There are a thousand things I could write about Fiona, but it's hard to put every little goosebump into words.

"Fiona"

## War

Feb. 24, 2015 | 5 y, 11 mo

Asking Finn what he learned today.

"Every time you go into war, you should go potty first." – Finn Tzu

"WAR!"

# 6

# **Six**cavators

## Battling incredulity

April 29, 2015 | 6 y, 1 mo

We should have named him Finnegan because we're always telling him, again and again, to do this or that. At one point this evening, I pleaded with Finn ... again. "Please, for the love of Star Wars, FOCUS!" Eventually he settled down and went to bed, where I broke out the dream journal.

Finn: "I don't want to tell a story tonight."

Me: "Let's do something different then. How are you feeling?"

Finn: "Uhh ..."

Me: "How's your heart? ... I mean, how do you feel about life, the universe and everything?"

Finn [grinning]: "I'm feeling focused!"

I can't complain about the sarcasm. They say it was my love for Scooby-Doo, but I suspect the real reason my parents called me Darby-Doo is because they were constantly telling me "Darby, do this. Darby, do that." They thought I wasn't focusing, but if anything, I was hyperfocusing on the mysteries of the universe. Finn's so far out in outer space sometimes, you have to poke him to get him to snap back to Earth.

Me: "It's about time. What are you focusing on?"

Finn: "I like to focus on schoolwork, except for art. But yesterday, in art class, they had Legos and I'm so happy that I built a sculpture. Sculpture Legos are the best type of Legos in the whole entire galactic galaxy. I really want to buy them."

Me: "Keep doing your chores and you'll be able to afford them. What else do you focus on?"

Finn: "I don't like to focus on music class."

Me: "Really? Why? I thought you liked to sing? You're really good, almost perfect pitch."

My fatherly pride is battling incredulity: How could my genes allow such insolence?

Finn: "I do like to sing, but all the songs are dumb. They're all about being healthy. Everybody wants to be healthy, but nobody wants to sing about being healthy."

Me: "Hahahaha! I know! Who wants to sing about going to bed early and eating vegetables, right!?"

I didn't tell Finn that night, but They Might Be Giants actually has a great children's album with songs about going to bed early and eating your vegetables. I totally sing along.

Fiona: "Why does my bib say 'Sweet-ass pie'?"

For a second I wonder if I actually bought this abomination. Finn's cracking up as he leans over and looks at the picture.

Finn: "It doesn't say 'Sweet-ass pie.' It says 'Sweet as pie.'"

Fiona: "Hahaha!"

Me: "Right. And 'Ass' like a donkey is spelled A-S-S. It's probably good to know the difference."

Speaking of life lessons ... yesterday, while driving home from Thanksgiving break:

Finn: "Why the heck is that restaurant named Pepé's? That is the strangest name for a restaurant!"

Finn's perplexed, eagerly awaiting a good explanation because he thinks "Pepé" actually means penis.

Perhaps the origin of this meaning goes back to his earliest years. Over time, "Pee-pee" must have evolved into a proper noun/pet name. Or maybe a certain parental figure planted this little joke early on to see how funny it would grow to be. I claim no superior knowledge. The logical explanation is that he learned the sound symbolism naturally during infancy. Let's go with that.

Me: "Huh. That is strange."

Finn is disappointed at my lame response, but still thoroughly amused. He chuckles, keeping his little inside joke to himself because, after all, there are ladies in the van.

Me: "Strange indeed."

This joke has been incubating for a while now. It's a long game, but it'll pay dividends when one of his friends has to break it to him. I've never let a practical joke stew this long, but when it lands, it'll be epic.

Fast forward:

November 22, 2023

I asked the boy awhile back if his friends ever confronted him about the pet name. He just laughed, but I couldn't get the story out of him. At least he's still getting a chuckle out of it. And he doesn't hate me, which is good. It was a risk I had to take. Planting seeds of embarrassment is an important part of parenting. It builds character and thickens the skin. I should really write a self-help book.

## The greatest thing I can teach you
Oct. 25, 2015 | 6 y, 7 mo

Driving to school. Running late … again.

Fiona: "Say you're sorry."

Me: "I was just doing my job. Remember? I'm a dad."

Fiona: "Say you're sorry and then I'll say sorry."

Me: "It doesn't work that way. You misbehaved. I don't want you to think that you can be mean to someone and then turn around and ask them to say sorry when you feel bad about it."

Fiona: "Why would I turn around?"

Me: "I don't know. Maybe you're fighting with someone and doing the hokey-pokey at the same time. It doesn't matter. Listen, you owe us an apology, not the other way around."

Fiona: "Sorry for not giving Finn privacy. [Now shouting.] But you need to say sorry too!"

Me: "Again, that's not the way it works."

Fiona: "Well, then you need to say something to make me happy, so I don't go to school with tears."

Me: "Oh, right. That's also my job. Sorry. Okay ... happy. Well the sun is shining. The sky is blue. When you think about the earth and all the stars in space, it makes our problems seem ... so little. When you think about all the big problems in the world, our problems become tiny."

[Fiona sighs]

Me: "See that right there – what you just did? You changed your mind. You started thinking about something else. Doesn't that feel nice? You can change your mind every day. That might be the greatest thing I can teach you."

For a few minutes, our drive to school is quiet, almost serene.

Finn: "Good speech."

Me: "Thanks. Alright, get out of the car or you'll be late!"

## When I die

Oct. 27, 2015

Dear dude in the big black truck who stopped at the crosswalk, as you would expect any evolved monkey to do, and then proceeded to gun it through a school zone, blowing past me (I was the one holding the giant rainbow-colored umbrella) and another guy (in the bright yellow rain jacket holding a big red stop sign in front of your face):

**I hope you were rushing to save somebody's life, because you almost ended mine.**

What the fuck dude? You stopped. Then all of a sudden, I was a few feet away from your grill. When I die, I hope that I come back as a bird, and I mean a big bird, so that I can take a ginormous steaming dump on your stupid black truck … daily.

Sincerely,
Future Blue Heron


## Peanuts!

Nov. 6, 2015 | 6 y, 8 mo

Me: "I'm gonna have to take out all the Snickers in your Halloween bag, buddy,"

Finn: "What!? Why?"

Me: "Peanuts." [They upset his tummy.]

Finn: "Can I say a cuss word right now?"

Me: "No."

Finn: "Peanuts!"

Me: [laughing]: "Hey, watch your mouth!"

## Origami breakfast
Dec. 10, 2015 | 6 y, 9 mo

Melina: "Why are you taking a picture of a pickle?"

Finn: "It's not a pickle. It's origami Emperor Pickletine."

Finn ate Emperor Pickletine for breakfast. The Force is strong with the boy.

## Pick up the pieces
Jan. 22, 2016 | 6y, 10 mo

We made the biggest snowman EVER ... almost. The kids and I started rolling at the top of a big hill at the end of our street and before long, the thing was massive. The snow was so sticky that when Finn and Fiona pushed, it stuck to their gloves and swiped 'em right off their hands. We couldn't catch up because gravity was happening.

The giant snow-butt engulfed their gloves and rolled all the way down the hill.

At the bottom where it flattened out, the ball was twice as big as it had been moments before.

The gloves were gone and none of us were prepared to do open-butt surgery on Frosty. It took everything in me to move the giant mass out of the middle of the street. The snowball was five feet in diameter! As

I rolled the ball out of the road one last time, it tipped over, hit the ground hard, and shattered into pieces.

"NOOOOOOOO!!!" I screamed. That was the kids' cue to laugh at me. Hank scampered up the tree and even stopped to ridicule me, "Squeheheheheeeee!"

"Stupid squirrel! I hope you forget where you buried your nuts!"

So I picked up all the pieces and built a snow monument – like one of those rock piles people stack along riversides. On the bright side, I ended up finding the kids' gloves in the snow, which made me think of the old proverb: You can't have your glove if the snowbutt eats it too.

Snowbutt: 0. Me: 1.

"Jones family snow day"

# 7

# **Seven**dipity

## Incredibly annoying

Mar. 28, 2016 | 7 y, 0 mo

Driving home to Nashville from North Carolina. Fiona's making a racket.

Finn: "Fiona, will you stop?"

Me: "Fiona, that's incredibly annoying? It's not funny."

[Continued cacophony]

Darby and Finn [shouting]: "Fiona!!!"

I glance back as she blows her last raspberry, which then morphs into a motorboat. She's still completely oblivious to our pleas, but questions my stink eye.

Fiona: "What? I'm covering my ears so I don't have to hear myself."

## Über embarrassed
April 7, 2016 | 7 y, 0 mo

On the way to school.

Zahra [neighbor kid]: "Your car is stinky."

[Both neighbor sisters laugh. I look in the rearview mirror. Finn and Fio look über embarrassed.]

Me: "Hahaha. You're right, but I think it's actually that black car in front of us. It's letting out some dirty smoke."

Fiona: "It's like it just farted on us."

[Kids laugh. The black car starts to turn right.]

Finn: "Now its butt cheek is blinking!"

## Red exclamation marks
Oct. 16, 2016 | 7 y, 7 mo

Finn and Fiona's friend and neighbor Zahra left abruptly to go tell her parents about our bathroom experience.

Finn: "I can't believe Zahra turned the bidet on full blast."

Me: "Hahahahaha. Oh my goodness! How do you know?"

Finn: "She said she did. She said she was gonna use it. And then we heard her scream."

Me: "Gosh, she's so tiny. I'm surprised it didn't blast her off the launch pad."

Fiona: "She could have been the first kid on the moon."

Finn: "I told her next time don't ignore the red exclamation marks."

## Hot red pants

Dec. 26, 2016 | 7 y, 9 mo

Hanging with cousins. Fio takes me aside.

Fio: "You're embarrassing me. First, you're wearing girl pants. Second, you're basically naked. You need to get dressed. Take these off!"

Me: "Right. Those are all valid points. But it's Christmas and these are the only hot red pants in the house. So I'm breaking down the … uh … girl/boy barriers for the cause. These are not girl pants today. They're Christmas pants and they fit nicely, if I do say so myself."

Fio: "Daaaad …"

Me: [slowly shutting the door on Fio]: "Nice and stretchy …"

Fio: "Dad!"

Me: "… and I'm only half naked!"

Fio: "DAD!!!"

Me: "I'm working on it."

Fio: "Thank you."

## I'm a big burrito

April 14, 2017

Yesterday morning was the last leg of a four-day trip to Las Vegas. After my conference concluded, I had a minute to lounge around the pool.

A little Hispanic girl, maybe 4 years old, jumped into the hammock next to mine and started singing as loud as she could, "I'm a little taco! I'm a little taco!"

It was so stinkin' adorable. Too adorable.

Not to be outdone, I quickly wrapped the tortilla shell (tan canvas hammock) around my entire body and operatically (à la Chevy Chase) mimicked her melody singing, "I'm a big burrito! I'm a big burrito!"

La chiquita y su madre laughed and laughed. Next, my feet slid out of the "burrito" and started conducting, cueing the little girl to resume her part.

La chiquita: "I'm a little taco! I'm a little taco!"

Me: "I'm a big burrito! I'm a big burrito!"

Our call and response lasted for a while, but we couldn't keep the deadpan going, so we both laughed and then said adios.

What fun! I was rolling my r's and everything. Thankfully, there weren't any social justice warriors nearby to accuse me of cultural appropriation.

"How dare that Ginger imitate a burrito like that!"

# 8

# Eight Going on **30**

## My little men

Oct. 21, 2017 | 8 y, 7 mo

Me and the boys go to Sloco on 12th Avenue South to eat manwiches and play Giant Jenga. This evening, Finn and his buddy William scarf their food and run outside like Tasmanian devils, but stop in their tracks to find a sweet little thing playing with "their" Jenga blocks. Will and Finn both look confused. They should be disappointed. Instead, they feel something entirely new.

When the little girl looks up, they quickly jump onto a nearby garden wall. Their parkour skills help them avoid an awkward stare, but more importantly show off their daring feats of strength and agility. After leaping from wall to window sill, they traverse across a bike rack. At this point, William turns back and says, "Hey, can we play?"

"Atta boy," I say under my breath.

All the kids look at me, and I pretend to clear my throat. "Sure," the young lady answers as she begins to stack the fallen blocks. She works quickly, with precision, building straight symmetric walls, careful not to step on the hem of her delicate dress, which has shiny iridescent flowers woven into the silver fabric. The boys jump in and before long their tower is too tall for them to reach. Not so for their new friend though. She has an extra inch, and a few more on tippytoes. She gracefully places the last block on top en pointe.

As they admire their work, Finn says, "Let's just take a moment to enjoy this." I about double over but keep my composure, so as not to embarrass the boys but mostly to steady the camera. Finn hasn't fully mastered deadpan yet, and his subtle grin gives away the sarcasm. Soon enough, the other two look at him and see the smirk.

"My name is Cadence," the little girl laughs. The boys introduce themselves too and then they go right back to their game. Cadence always plays it safe while the boys deliberately make their tower as precarious as possible. Several crashes later, William has had enough. "OK, let's go home now and start our YouTube channel."

Finn looks perplexed. His smile is saying that he wants to stay, but his eyes dart back and forth, questioning whether to play with friend or female. Finally he relaxes. "One more game isn't that long … in the grand scheme of things."

"THAT'S MY BOY!!!" I think. But my mental exclamation points manifest into a low guttural sound that everyone hears. They look at me again. "No [cough]. It's not a long time. Go play."

Instead of playing another game, they decide to write out in giant Jenga block letters, "I Heart Sloco!" and walk on the words like a balance beam. Cadence treads with purpose, straight as an arrow until she gracefully lifts her arms, pivots, and twirls into a perfect pirouette.

**Her dress twirls up in the air, then floats down as she looks right at the boys. They don't know what centrifugal motion is, but it renders them speechless.**

Finally the awkward silence breaks. "It's time to go, Sweetie," reminds a motherly voice. Cadence immediately obeys, but meanders slowly away.

I whisper, "Hey, buddy. This is generally the time when people say, 'It was a pleasure meeting you.'" Finn says "Bye," but nobody hears him over 12th Avenue traffic. Finn looks at me, silently asking, "What next?" I nod toward the young lady's family, still sitting at their table. My eyes say, "It's obvious man!" Finn opens his eyes wide as if to say, "I tried!?" I shrewdly lower my left eyebrow while raising my right, thus winning the facial expression argument with a simple yet effective, "Really?" He turns in defeat and walks up to Cadence and her family.

I wasn't sure if he'd do it, but Finn faces his fear, takes a deep breath, and says, "We had fun playing with you, Cadence. Goodbye." The family, all 10 of them, stare. It's the mom who turns red, though; Cadence is too confident to blush. She's not surprised. She had a great time. Her smile is a simple recognition of satisfaction. Both mother and daughter say goodbye in unison … to my little men.

## Black hole
2018

I'm pretty sure 2018 fell into a black hole. Tweenager censors crashed the party, so they aren't talking as much. Looks like you're stuck with me.

"Mwahahahahahaaaaa!"

## Halloween

Oct. 31, 2018

Parents can take my candy all night long, but if they're not dressed up, they ain't dipping their hands into my pumpkin. It's not that hard. A single rubber band is all it takes to be terrifying.

Time to make little kids cry.

# 9

# And Now for Something
## Completely Different

As I mentioned, the kids are a bit touchy these days. Something about hormones blah blah blah. So until they learn to make fun of themselves, I'm going to steal the mic.

### Depression
Sept. 21, 2019

If I ever encounter major depression, I wouldn't get a therapy dog. I don't want to put that kind of pressure on a puppy to perform and keep me happy. I'd be more likely to hire an emotional support clown.

And I'd pay double if the clown arrived each day on this pink elephant.

## Sick feeling
Dec. 20, 2019

Whenever I'm driving and someone honks, I immediately think that it's me, that I've left a glass coffee mug on the roof ... again.

Sometimes people will drive by laughing, looking in my direction and I get the same sick feeling. Then I remember that my license plate says "NIBLETS. " It's either that or I've left a glass coffee mug on the roof ... again.


## Keto cups
Jan. 20, 2020

Mel got Keto Cups today. They're supposed to be comparable to Reese's Cups, right? Of course, the Whole Foods version is all organic, vegan, gluten-free, no sugar added, made with almond butter, artichoke fiber, and monk fruit (whatever that is).

Incredibly, they taste exactly like Reese's Cups ... that is if a dog ate and evacuated said Reese's Cups into your mouth.

They cost four times as much, but totally worth every penny when you get quality shit like that.


## Covid side effects
May 5, 2020

It's lockdown, day three of wearing the same black pants and blue shirt to reduce our laundry footprint. We're fiddling around in the garden, waiting for the edibles to kick in. It's been a few days since I smelled like I needed a shower. Oh no! I think I've caught it. I'm turning into a hippie.

# Craigslist bunk bed

June 10, 2020 | 9 y, 3 mo

My quest to get the kids a bunk bed started one Sunday evening with an ATM machine that was out of service. It was no big deal. I had plenty of time before I needed to meet up with the family I had contacted on Craigslist. Next, I drove to U-Haul to pick up the rental van.

I had already checked in online, so when I walked up to the front desk, it only took a minute before Jesse, the U-Haul guy, said "Let's go" – the key word being "let's." I figured that meant he was right behind me, but as I walked outside, I was alone … for five long minutes.

So then I power-walked back inside and saw Jesse searching under a desk, looking on the wall, merrily cavorting around. The entire time he was whistling between his teeth like the goddamn Gopher from Winnie the Pooh. And why not? He told me I was his last customer, so he was sooooo close to not giving a shit.

This thought cheered me up. I wished I could whistle like Gopher. Then I snapped out of my Hundred Acre Wood dream sequence and asked, "Hello? What's going on here?"

Ten unproductive minutes later I sent a courtesy text to the family, notifying them that I was running a little late. Meanwhile, Jesse pulled out a cigar box full of keys and slowly went through them one by one, flipping the keys over, while nonchalantly saying "Nope." Or sometimes, "Noooo?" I called those false-hope-nopes. Clearly, I had plenty of time to categorize the sounds coming out of his face.

Eventually, Jesse gave up and started to set me up with another van. Just as we signed the papers, did the hokey pokey, and turned ourselves around, up drove a giant rental truck, which had to double-park since the lot was completely full.

Next, a lady looking just as annoyed as I was got out and stormed into the building. That's when Jesse informed me that my rental van was one of several vehicles stuck between parking blocks and a big-ass truck.

60

Before I could ask the lady to move the truck, she started raising hell; something about her phone calls getting forwarded to Corporate. Between her bouts of bitching, the lady asked how Jesse's family was doing and they discussed other matters of vital importance like their favorite colors and what Jesse's cat puked up.

Another representative heard the commotion and walked over to help. Both reps had completely forgotten that I existed, so I snapped. "Hey! One person can deal with her and another one can get me the hell out of here!!!"

Jesse could tell that I was frustrated, so he proceeded to ask if his supervisor would mind driving my rental van over the parking block, off the curb of the street, and into oncoming rush-hour traffic. The supervisor told Jesse to "fuck off" (politely, I'll admit) and continued to get harangued because he didn't have the authority to make the lady's late penalties disappear.

So Jesse metaphorically grabbed himself by the balls and strutted out like a boss. He didn't need no stinking permission! Before I could bat an eye, he had the van cranked up. Now, rush hour traffic in Nashville is stupid, but Jess hopped the curb like a gypsy cab driver in Manhattan, flipped off oncoming traffic, and expertly navigated to a spot where I could hop in for the getaway.

Jessie jumped out and tossed me the keys, which wasn't very professional, but totally badass. I could have hugged the scruffy-looking teenager, but he didn't give me a chance. Jessie turned and bee-lined it over to a beater Honda civic. His day was done. He was ready to sail off into a six pack and some Taco Bell.

"Fuckin' A," I said, as a salute to my man Jessie.

Finally, I was on the road, truckin', searching for an ATM (that worked this time). I couldn't help but feel sort of slap-happy and amused. Thankfully, there was a grocery store with an ATM on the way, so I stopped in and grabbed the cash.

I was 30 minutes late for the pickup, so I sprinted across the parking lot, still in getaway mode. Back at the van, I leaped into the seat and landed the key into the ignition in one fluid motion. I was feeling pretty badass myself, until I heard someone directly behind me shout "Hey!"

"That's weird," I thought. "Why are there people in my van?" Then I look back and see two wide-eyed teenagers wearing the same what-the-fuck face as me. And exactly two parking spaces over was a very similar looking white van. Except it wasn't. My van had a huge fucking fish jumping out of the water. The van I was in had people in it.

I tried to stutter out an apology but the teenagers just stared blankly with their mouths open. So I jumped out, hopped into the "fraternal twin" rental van and skedaddled. I looked over and the teens were laughing their asses off, clearly elated that I was just a dumbass and not an abductor.

The sunset was wild, which made the drive through Sumner County pleasant. Instead of speeding to get somewhere a little less than really late, I took it 10 mph under the limit, rolled down the windows, and breathed in the fresh country air. That lasted for a few breaths before a big pick-up truck with smelly exhaust turned in front of me.

Towering above me, about three times the height of the trailer and not ratchet-strapped down was a massive pile of branches, limbs, and logs. So instead of enjoying the beautiful countryside, my eyes were glued to the back of a trailer, watching a pile of wood bounce and teeter off the sides, hoping not to get hit by falling debris.

In the end, I made it back home in time to enjoy the end of the sunset. The kids fit snugly into their new bunk bed. Finn and Fiona were excited to have their first big-kid bed, and were extra huggable.

That's all they'll remember. And that's all that matters.

## Ol' Red

Aug. 24, 2020

Goodbye, Gramps. You had 90 wonderful years, 70 with Grandma. Gonna miss hearing your stories about life on the farm, the pranks on your dad and the two cows that you tied together. Kids had to find amusements while they worked, six long days a week. You only had a short time on Sunday between church and dinner to play.

Everything you did was for your family, and you passed that on to us all. You had a thirst for knowing what was going on around you: reading the Dayton Daily front to back and sharing the knowledge with anyone who'd sit down and listen. You were always there for us. It gave you such pleasure to visit and talk about the rain, work, kids – all the while, nonstop weather updates or country music would play in the background. I always looked up to you as a family man. I hope to live up to your love.

Sorry that I couldn't say goodbye in person, but I hope you liked the last tune that I played over the phone. Right afterwards, uncle Roger told me that you went home in the middle of the chorus.

I guess "Amazing Grace" was either the last thing you wanted to hear, or my rendition was so bad that dying was the easiest way to make it stop.

I'm just messing with you Gramps. I know you liked it.

Thanks for giving me your locks and for not going bald. You're still looking good. Love ya, Red!

# 10

# Flight **Club**

## How to make love to a tree

Aug. 29, 2020

Shasta. It's a river, a lake, a tribe. It's a place that adventurers and travelers who have seen it all call home.

Shhhastaaaa. I like to say it. The last time Shasta said anything explosive was in 1786, but the people of Shasta blew up when Nestlé tried to move in and tap her headwaters for bottled water. They ran 'em out of town and kept their water pure. Shasta is a way of life.

Not that the people are opposed to honest industry. They're home to Shasta, the 125-year-old value-priced soft drink. And just like the people, their brand is unique, with offerings like Grapefruit Zazz, Orange Creamsicle, Bubble Gum, and Candy Cane Cola. The soda is still popular today and best enjoyed while listening to '80s New Wave synthpop (any Ministry fans?). Al Jourgensen wrote Shasta's jingle.

"Jourgensen Jingle"

If you're still not convinced of Shasta's superlative soda, just ask The Beastie Boys. They'll tell you.

"I'm the master blaster, drinking up the Shasta, my voice sounds sweet cause it hasta."

Taking it back to 1992, that's "Professor Booty" from the album Check Your Head.

So what's the point of all the trivia? Where do we go now? Or, a more interesting question: Where did we come from?

Mount Shasta is the place where I entered the motherfucking universe. I was born 3,600 feet above sea level on the flanks of a volcano.

I don't remember anything from my childhood in northern California, but our family photo album was vivid enough. One of my favorite faded old photographs is of my family wearing bathing suits in the snow. At higher elevations, blizzards at night, then 70 degree weather the next day was not uncommon. There weren't any snowmen around, but there were definitely a few snowdudes chilling out when we left the mountain.

Surely this magical mountain had an effect on my love for nature and for getting lost … on purpose. At 40 years old, I'm still climbing trees. I remember wearing dress shoes and a cummerbund, but that didn't stop me. If I see a tree with some nice knobs and thick branches, it's on.

You might see me if I let you. You might hear an owl and say to yourself, "I thought owls sleep during the day?" Then you'll look up and be like, "What the fuck dude? Everyone's waiting. Aren't you the best man?" All this is perfectly normal in my world. And my hoot is dead on.

When I was a kid, my friend Jake taught me how to use my hands to "whistle like the Indians," but I perfected the technique. Basically you cup your hands together and blow straight down into a little hole you make between your thumbs. To get the owl's purring sound just right, you exhale and gargle simultaneously. Fluctuating the pitch is just like playing a trombone. Just slide a few fingers up and down to get the right sound. That's it! That's how I roll.

I do a lotta stuff in trees, which brings us to the title of the story. It's not a metaphor.

This is an account of how to make love to a tree, properly, 6,950 ft above sea level. Most trees won't turn you down, so it's a much easier way to join the Mile High Club.

Before my big adventure, my last glimpse of Shasta was from my cradle. Twenty years later, I decided to go on a pilgrimage to my place of origin. I planned the trip with my faerie friend, Meaghan Owens. She was a fellow songwriter and adventurer who I was secretly in love with. Everyone who meets Meaghan falls in love, so it's not a big secret.

Anyways, back in Nashville, I told Meaghan that I was planning to move to California in a few months to start a music publishing company. She was like, "Oh that's cool. I'll be in Mt. Shasta around then."

Me: "No way. That's where I was born!"

Meaghan: "Really?

Me: "Yeah, I'll be in Oakland for a bit, but I was planning to make my way up to Shasta at some point."

Meaghan: "You should come visit!"

Meaghan was going to Shasta to visit Lucy, the mother of her late friend Sequoya. Lucy's son Shannon lived in San Francisco. I hadn't met him before, but Meaghan said we'd be best of friends. Since my sister Willow lived in Oakland, I decided to fly out and see them both. After a quick visit with Willow, Shannon and I took off in his beater car and headed north.

My friend Sharon also lived nearby, but she can be a little flaky, so I gave her barely enough time to pack, but not enough time to think about the consequences of a big decision. It worked, so Shannon (dude) and Sharon (dudette) joined forces and we all took off.

According to Oatmeal Muncher University, Shasta is Earth's root chakra, "the access point to 'All That Is,' a place where you are bathed in knowingness and nurtured by the realization and frequency of oneness."

Sounds a little woo-woo, but "Woo-hoooo!" We were on a road trip!

One flat tire and a lotta laughs later, we arrived. It must have been around midnight, but Meaghan was there to welcome us as soon as we stepped out of the car.

I remember seeing every star in the sky. The Milky Way was so vivid that it looked like a cirrus cloud stretching from one horizon to the other. As I gave Meaghan a big bear hug, lifting her up off my mountain, a shooting star streaked across the sky over her shoulder. Shannon saw it too.

The next day, we all headed up to Bunny Flat, 6,950 feet up the south side of the mountain. As soon as we hit the trail head, we all went silent. Everything was covered in snow, glittering in sunbeams shining through California Furs. One beam illuminated a little old man, bald with fluffy white sideburns. He had a burlap bag in one hand and was sprinkling seeds with the other. Two white butterflies fluttered around him.

"Did someone spike my oatmeal?" I wondered. "Is this happening?" Then he looked right at us and said, "Would you like to help?"

I couldn't even process all the data streaming in, but I knew the right answer was "YES!"

All my existential dilemmas vanished. Spreading beauty across the earth is exactly what I wanted to do with my life. We lost track of time sprinkling wildflower seeds, wandering through the woods until we had essentially become the butterfly effect and our hunger pangs had long given up trying to remind us of lunch.

At last we group-hugged with the old man and took off to search for the perfect place in the snow to spread our picnic blanket. The faded family photograph that had captured my childish curiosity was no longer a dream.

It was at this point that Sharon decided to announce, "Oh, by the way, my boyfriend goes to these, like, mind-expansion conferences in Switzerland, so he knows some of the scientists who attend. Anyway, it's probably not going to work out between us because he's like this weird idiot savant. It's a tough decision though, because he always has good shit. […] One Smiley Face for you. One for you. You can have the Jesus Lizard. We can split the Posh Monkey down the middle if you want."

For the next six hours, words and laughter became one and the same.

We feasted on purple scones with blackberry jam and cream. We had crispy cheese'n'onion hogbake, trifles, candied chestnuts, rhubarb pie with apple snow. Of course we washed it down with Shasta's own Summer Strawberry Fizz. I might have made up the apple snow bit, but my friends looked like woodland critters at the time, so let's just say it was hard to distinguish between real and Redwall.

After we had our fill, Shannon and I took off on our own adventure, running as fast as we could up the steep slope. Next, I remember lying flat on my back on a fallen tree, trying and failing to catch my breath. Capturing ephemeral mist is much harder than it looks, so I decided to let it be, and gaze through the icy smoke, focusing intently on the neon green moss growing on the limbs above. As I moved my head out of a shadow into the sunlight, I closed my eyes, whereupon the entire forest remained clear and colorful, only imprinted under my eyelids. To this day, I can still see these impressions. Whenever I need clarity or wisdom, my dreams will take me back to the exact spot, to my Castanadian place of power.

When I opened my eyes, I spotted a clearing off to my right through the woods about 100 feet away. The expanse was uninhabited except for one lone evergreen tree in the middle. She was beautiful, but had a little imperfection: an offshoot limb growing sideways from her base. I didn't mind. She was a tall, skinny young thing and I was gonna mount her. I mean, I was going to ask if I could climb first.

I walked over and sat on the offshoot, which made for a nice bench – strong, yet flexible. As I bounced, I wasn't sure if an idea was growing in my mind or if my mind was growing on the idea. In any case, we grew on each other until I jumped up off the branch and ran a bit further up the mountain. After a big exhale, my breath disappeared and I took off again, this time barreling down the slope. As I approached the tree, I crouched low and leaped onto the limb, springing off with all my might, then flying seven or eight feet through the air, screaming from the shock of it all. Shannon had to help dig me out of the snow hole that I made from the impact.

I perfected my flying squirrel impression for what felt like half a day (in LSD time). In reality though, we were Greenwich mean minus eight, sooooo … give or take a few lunar seconds it was probably about … five minutes.

I was doing flips and twists and triple Salchows. It didn't matter if I landed on my feet or my hands or my head. There was sooooo much snow to soften the blow. Shannon just sat and watched, occasionally helping to pull me out of a hole.

Finally, when I was too tired to go on, I jumped into the evergreen and gave my new lady friend a big bear hug. She seemed to like that, so I disappeared into her branches as I whispered all the things that I wanted to do to her. I won't say what she whispered back, but it was nasty.

A few moments later, Shannon saw me pop up out at the very top, 40 feet up. He immediately sprang to his feet and yelled for me to get down. I politely hollered, "When the time is right!" It was a convincing argument, apparently, because he just shook his head and sat back down. If I plummeted to death, at least he could say that he tried.

At that height I could see all the way down the mountain. Off to the North, neon streaks of light kept flashing by. I thought I was just hallucinating. Shannon told me they were local skiers on the slopes nearby.

Straight ahead and southwest of Shasta, about eleven miles away, was Mount Eddy, which sat in a long mountain range that stretched across the horizon. The cumulus clouds above looked like a mirror image of the mountains below.

I could see my breath engulfing the tiny cones at the top of my tree. Most evergreens have cones that hang down, but hers curved upward, a trait unique to Shasta's California Fir. The baby cones at the top were so soft, like velvet to the touch.

We were swaying effortlessly. Next thing you know, I was rocking back and forth to the natural rhythm and sound of the wind. Before long we were careening three feet this way, five feet that way, then six, seven, eight feet in either direction.

Shannon yelled, "Darby, be careful!" but I was carefree, riding that tree like a composer orchestrating the earth as I hurled its weight in each direction. In that moment we became one – literally, one giant pendulum of a metronome, having the time of our lives.

I was 30 feet high, screaming like a banshee at my shadow, "Try and catch me now!" But she couldn't keep up with our tempo.

"Oh my god! Full on double mountain across the sky! [sobbing] What does it mean?!" I sounded like Bear, the double rainbow dude from Yosemite.

"Double Rainbow"

I don't know if the universe gave Bear an answer, but what I think the double rainbow means is that life is beautiful, and you have to be present or you might miss it.

"Booyakasha!" I screamed. It's an Irish saying that means high glory and love to the very moment. I usually reserve the exclamation for winning game point in badminton, but I literally felt like the birdie floating to and fro, so it was totally called for.

I can imagine the skiers doing a double-take and skidding to a hockey stop to gawk. Obviously, some of it was performance on my part. There's a certain thrill you get when you know people are watching and boy were there some bright flashing lights watching me get it on that day.

I remember the thick musky smell of her sap, the way it felt smeared all over my face. I didn't wash her off for days. Or, wait … actually, it *wouldn't* wash off. I tried, but it was too sticky for consumer-grade soap. It doesn't matter. The consummation of love should be sticky.

The level of love we made that day has surely ruined me. "Oh my God," I thought. "Please don't end. Please …" But it was time. I made the choice, laid back and fell. I didn't think about it, just instinctively knew that it was possible because my mind had previously stored crucial data, namely that my young California Fir's green branches were supple enough to bend but not break. I don't remember recalling this construct explicitly. The knowledge was simply encoded into my subconscious, as if the physics of the fall was part of me.

Each branch was a little longer than the branch above, so they all "caught" me before delivering me to the branch below until I rolled off the tree into a big pillow of snow. I laid there and stared in wonder, strangely craving a cigarette. I didn't even smoke, but the urge seemed normal.

It was a dream. It happened. Shannon nearly shat his pants and told everyone when we got back. Then he told everyone again the next day – when I could finally distinguish words from sound effects. He's probably still telling the story to this day.

I'll leave you now with some lyrics inspired by the mighty Shasta Mountain.

## Into the Wild

Guess it's goodbye. Time to fly
Jump off this high-wire act
No safety net. I'mma cheat death
Look forward to the impact

Cracked my lips on a total eclipse
I'll never see me again
Found some peyote. I'm a howling coyote
Hiding from the lawman

I'm heading …

Into the wild. I don't know where I'm going
Into the wild write'cha when I get there
Into the wild my sky domicile
Into the wild die with a smile

It ain't too late to make an escape
But soon you'll be stuck in your ways
So bring some money, ride the rails honey
You ain't lost if you love the maze

OW OW AHHOOOO!!!

Into the wild. I don't know where I'm going
Into the wild write'cha when I get there
Into the wild my sky domicile
Into the wild die with a smile

## Kinky cicadas
Sept. 20, 2020

Wikipedia calls it Flying Ant day, but if I was the editor, I would have totally gone with Nuptial Flight Club.

It's exactly what it sounds like. Every year, on a hot, sweaty day, swarms of flying ants launch straight up into the air and turn the sky into one giant aerial orgy. Wings shimmer and bodies crash into one big bang.

**I'm such a nerd. I get turned on watching bugs. There's a scientific word for it. It's called *entomology* — the study of *insex*.**

Sometimes, when conditions are really moist, it attracts so many flying ants that they resemble rain showers on weather radar systems. This means somewhere, a meteorologist is also getting turned on.

It's a big annual holiday for local birds as well. Depending on your point of view, Nuptial Flight Club is either feast or fuckin' – or both: a feast on the fuckin'.

After the deed is done, the prince's wings fall off and he drops dead. The queen also sheds her wings but does so strategically after landing, which settles the debate on which sex is smarter.

Then, for up to fifteen years, she'll lay eggs almost continuously, giving birth to an entire colony – hundreds of thousands of land roamers and air fuckers.

Imagine if you were the dudeant, though. You just laid the hottest queen babe in the air! Everything's cool. Then, all of a sudden, your wings fall off and you plummet to a gruesome death. Way to take one for the team, buddy.

Here's some more insect S&M to ponder. Ms. Mantis will sometimes incorporate cannibalism into copulation. After she bites her lover's head off, Mr. Mantis continues to assume the position and finishes her off like a gentleman.

Proof that even decapitation can't kill the mood. What a good sport. Not many can say they went out doing what they loved. Speaking of which …

**The other day, I found two dead cicadas stuck together. It was the most romantic thing I'd ever seen. They stucked to death.**

So, being the weirdo that I am, it gave me an idea – only it came to me in a dream that woke me up around 3 a.m. The entire song was in my head.

This one's for all the kinky cicadas out there.

### Love Me to Death

The day we met, I gave you my life
Just a little girl, now I'm your wife
Never wanted to leave, but now I'm trying
'Cause it hurts to breathe – Doc says I'm dying

I don't know if there's a heaven above
I'm not religious – I believe in your love
You fell for me, guardian angel
Put a spell on me – *"You Are So Beautiful"*

Chorus
I'm barely here, but I can hear everythin'
I wanna feel your lips, don't need no medicine
I'll fit you into this hospital bed
Be one with me, *mi amore* before I'm dead

Before I pass into oblivion
Lay your head, hear my heart's rhythm
Won't you grant me my last request
Kiss me goodbye and love me to death

Chorus
I'm barely here, but I can hear everything
I wanna feel your lips, don't need no medicine
I put my lipstick on – the cherry red
I'll leave my mark before I'm dead

Baby, come quick – I fell on the floor
I'm losing breath – give me yours
Don't help me up – lay right here
Whisper your love in my ear

Chorus
I'm barely here, but I can hear everythin'
I feel your lips. I feel your medicine
As my heart departs let us profess
our love. Lay me to rest

In peace … loved to death
In peace … loved to death

Maybe insects have it right. Their whole lives revolve around one improbable instinct — to connect before it's too late. We call it love. They call it life.

In the end, we're all just trying to love each other to death.

## Butterfly dreams

Oct. 15, 2020

"Oh no!!! Is she … ?"

A moment earlier, everything was peaceful and serene. It was a cool spring morning. I was lying on a quilt my grandma made, listening to the brook running through our backyard. That's when I saw her.

I had to stretch, but I could just barely see the tips of her wings as they moved slowly in and out of view behind a patch of grass. If you ever see a butterfly flex like this, they're not just flapping their wings idly. Everything they do has a purpose. This little dance is meant to seduce a worthy suitor. And since I didn't see any other butterflies around, my ego and I were pretty sure she was putting on a show for us.

But we wanted to see all of her, not just a piece. Something told me to let it be, but I ignored it. Not only that, but I was too lazy to get off my ass, so I picked up a rock and threw it in the general vicinity, hoping the noise would stir the creature into flight. However, instead of throwing a strike on the outer edge of the plate, I accidentally hit the batter. "Oh no!!!"

I didn't see her moving. "Is she …?"

I jumped up to confirm my suspicion, but it was too terrifying, so I woke up abruptly, breathing heavily, heart pounding. I basically got kicked out of my dream for being an asshole – for murdering a butterfly.

"What the hell does that mean?" I wondered. But honestly, I didn't want to know, so I decided to phone a friend. I knew my buddy Josh could calm me down. I must have woken him up, because he sounded annoyed; told me to chill. "Buddy, why don't you roll over to my place and we'll talk about it," he relented.

When I got to Josh's, he made some coffee and we went outside to enjoy the rest of the morning. He had a lovely front yard in a hip neighborhood near Belmont, where I went to school. It was all landscaped with trestles full of flowers, just starting to bloom.

"And then I woke up" were the words floating out of my mouth as I threw my hands up in the air. Josh's eyes were as wide as a pregnant woman's areolas.

I thought I was telling a good story, but that wasn't it. Spoken word has never been my forté. My mouth has never been patient enough for my mind to catch up. I'm only a decent writer 'cause I can slow it down enough for my brain to hang.

Back to the story. Before I could say another word, I swear on my grandmother's grave, a big yellow butterfly fluttered over my right shoulder and landed on my outstretched elbow.

Jaws dropped. Goosebumps sprouted as our neck hair stood erect. We were still as stalagmites.

"I've never had one land on me," I whispered.

A euphoric rush of endorphins surfed my spine and exploded in my skull. My fairy friend must have felt the surge of energy, because her wings began flitting wildly. At some point her wings accelerated such that she began hovering in place. Maybe one of my goosebumps pricked her. Then she flew around my head a few times and floated off. She had places to be, flowers to fertilize, dreams to catch.

Josh looked like a voyeur caught in the act. I was glad he was watching, though. I needed someone to vouch that I wasn't still in a dream; that I was consciously participating in reality.

Me: "You'll have to punch me cause a pinch won't do!"

"Ow! Dude, I was joking."

Josh: "See, man, she just dropped in [singing] to see what condition your condition was in."

Me: "Ha!"

Josh: "She wanted to make sure you were all right. She said it's all good man. Peace out motherfuckaaah."

I don't know what it means. Maybe nothing. It was just a dream. Or maybe at the time, there was something beautiful just ahead and I needed to be patient. Try and capture a delicate thing, and you might crush it.

Spring awakens

Caterpillar cocoons

Butterfly dreams

## The scariest night of my marriage
Nov. 8, 2020

Somehow, the scariest night of my life turned into the hardest I've ever laughed. That pretty much sums up our wedding and marriage in general … but also last Tuesday.

After watching Aliens the other night, I went to bed and dreamt I was in this weird Hunger Games competition, last-one-standing kinda thing, only it was set in a shopping mall and we weren't fighting people, just avoiding being mauled by roving gangs of cats. Every variety you can imagine: housecats, bobcats, sabre-tooth tigers. Garfield made a cameo, which really messed me up because he's supposed to make me laugh, not eat me.

Anyway, about the time that I hatched a plan to escape, I felt something crawl up my arm. Keep in mind, Aliens had set all this in motion, so I immediately thought it was one of those little face-suckers that run around like Thing from The Addams Family.

Meanwhile, in the real world, something scuttled across my face. I'm talking about a cockroach. La Cucaracha right across my eyeballs. Naturally, I screamed like a little girl and jumped out of bed.

Melina had felt something moments before, but her dream-mind decided to chalk it up to my hair tickling her arm. She may have ignored the warning from her inner self, but she could not ignore me screaming bloody murder. Out of a deep slumber, she flung the covers to the floor and somersaulted off the end of the bed.

It would have been olympic if she had stuck the landing, but her dismount looked like what it was: someone hurtling off a king-sized balance beam in the dark. There was just enough moonlight for me to see her crash to the floor.

I stood there in horror at the thought of a neck injury or concussion. To make matters worse, Melina started convulsing. The numbers 911 flashed across my mind until I realized she was doing another instinctual thing: giggling uncontrollably, and silently, the way you do because you need to fill your lungs with enough air before you can properly explode. Which she did. From the gut. And we went on like this, howling until our sides hurt so bad that we couldn't tell if the tears were from agony or hilarity.

What a great movie. Totally worth the terrifying nightmares.

Speaking of hilarious scares. This one was epic:

"Say hello to my little friend"

## WALL-E

Nov 21, 2020

So three training sessions and a pound of peanut butter later, my dog finally let herself in. Nudged the door open with her nose, and then turned right around and high-fived it shut.

I witnessed the feat from the comfort of my bed. I didn't have to get up, so I should have been happy, but my feelings quickly faded into a weird Orwellian dystopia. I felt like I did that day when the kids finally learned how to go number two on their own, as if nobody would need me anymore.

I hardly need me. Got a bidet that cleans my ass. Got a Roomba that cleans my house. I call him WALL-E because he likes his little home base by the wall where he returns to charge up. At least WALL-E needs me. I pull out the hair that gets stuck in his wheels and vacuum the dust from his air filter. It gets really filthy. WALL-E thinks using another vacuum to do this is embarrassing, but he lets me do it anyway. Probably feels good if you ask me. Of course I change his little bag and put him all back together.

Maybe one day he'll change my bag. I'm not entirely sure what that means, but what I think I'm saying is that I don't want another man to do it. I don't even want Melina to change my bag.

I think she's getting jealous. She won't admit it, but I think she hid WALL-E's attachment hose – like she's suspicious that there's something going on between us. But we're just friends – me and my WALL-E.

## Snow

Nov. 29, 2020

Reading Good News Network headlines.

For the First Time in History, AI Learns to Translate Silent Human Brain Activity into Text

Aaaand we're officially living in a science fiction movie. That's it. The robots can now translate the thoughts of paralyzed patients into words.

One of my fondest memories occurred after my grandma had a stroke and had to completely relearn how to speak. She was fully aware and understood us, but the only thing she could say was the word "snow." That was all I heard her say until the day I turned 19, when she came to celebrate and Grandpa taught her to sing "Happy Birthday." It was the sweetest gift I could have asked for.

I would give anything to have had one more long conversation with her. Now science and technology are making these "impossible" conversations a reality.

# 11

# Laughing **and** Crying

## Nirvāna

Dec. 5, 2020

**My first hitchhiking experience happened a few weeks after Mel and I found out we were having twins.**

I was driving from Nashville to Indianapolis to meet Mel at a Bob Dylan concert when I saw two hitchhikers sitting by the road. I didn't think about it; just stopped, rolled down the window, and said, "Hop in." I told the two young women where I was going, but they didn't seem to care. They were riding the wind.

After some small talk, I had to get it off my chest. I hadn't told anyone about the twins, so opening up to complete strangers was strange, but also cathartic. They talked me through some doubts that I wasn't sure how to convey to family and friends. I had always wanted to be a dad, but was afraid settling down meant sacrificing my dreams. Ever since I read Into The Wild, I wanted to march into the open country and live the hobohemian lifestyle. At least for a while.

Picking up a couple of free spirits was a spark, but their stories of adventure lit a fire under my ass. They urged me to take the leap, saying I could easily go on a short journey before the kids came.

Back in Nashville, I wrote an anthem to accompany my trip called "Free Ride Lullabye," but playing it felt like fraud. So I planned to unveil it after getting some street cred by hitching to the Frank Brown International Songwriters Festival. This was an annual pilgrimage to the Gulf Shores. But I had always attended as a fan. My plan had to get me there on time this year, my first year as an artist, or I risked burning bridges that had taken years to build. In particular, I had always dreamed of performing at the legendary Florabama, likely the biggest roadhouse in the South. No way could I let this crazy idea screw it up.

All the festival's A-listers play the 'Bama, but around midnight, folks start trickling across the street to the River House, where the real magic happens. All the stars live there during the fest and jam around the kitchen table, or they shut up as one songwriter drops a tune that blows everyone away. The bombs drop all night until everyone is obliterated. That's where I needed to be.

On November 17, 2008, my journey began. Well, actually I cheated and got a ride to the highway. Melina wouldn't take me on principle, meaning she didn't want to play a role in some serial killer picking me up and selling my organs to China. Or something like that.

Since calling a taxi would be a terrible beginning to a story about hitchhiking, I decided to call our realtor. She found our Nashville home where we would raise the twins, and she was always on the go, so why not?

"Hey Ja'nay-nay, remember when you said to call anytime if I needed you? Well I was just checking the time and 'anytime' is right now." She picked me up immediately and told me not to get killed before she dropped me off on Old Hickory Boulevard.

The temperature was close to freezing at sunset and dropping fast. I didn't even make it off the 65 South entrance ramp before I got my first ride.

**She was young, attractive, had short blonde hair with a pretty smile, and the first thing she did was apologize.**

"I'm sorry, but I can only take you to Concord." I tilted my head back and laughed from my gut. Concord Road was only a few miles away. "Don't worry darlin'. This is the first time I've ever hitchhiked and it only took me a minute to catch my first ride. It's a good omen, and you'll get me one exit closer to the beach."

Her name was Leigh Ashby. She said she was new to Nashville; just moved from Winston-Salem. "That's cool," I said. "I have a friend named Mostafa who moved here from Winston-Salem. He studied film at the School of the Arts. She perked up, "MOSTAFA!? Crazy Moroccan dude with dreadlocks?"

Leigh parked on a side street and we traded stories about our mutual Moroccan. Before she left, she gave me a mix-CD that she had made especially for road trips. "I have friends who hitchhike," she said. "So when I saw you, I just felt called to help out." We parted on that thought.

I wasn't having much luck on Concord Road, so I decided to try the highway. My best friend Buzz once told me to walk backwards so people could see your face. It made sense, but even a professional vagabond like Buzz would find it difficult to walk backwards while holding a guitar and pulling a cheap suitcase with chincy wheels. I couldn't even stick my thumb out.

Out of necessity, I managed to push the guitar neck through the suitcase handle so it could ride on top. Freeing up one hand was great, but freeing up the thumb was an evolutionary triumph.

But none of it did me any good that night. By the time I could properly hitchhike, it was too dark and nobody could see my face. Right about the time my shoulders were starting to ache, someone pulled over. Finally, relief! I couldn't see anything through the headlights, though. And then, as I started to walk up, the driver got out. This was a little odd. That was when I realized the guy was a cop. He told me it was illegal to walk along the highway if I was hitchhiking and said he'd give me a ticket if he saw me past the next exit.

It's only two miles to Moores Ln, but by the time I got there my shoulders were in bad shape. I regretted not getting a gig bag with shoulder straps. Hell, I really didn't need a guitar anyway; there would be hundreds to choose from at the festival. Losing my guitar would have been a bad idea though. A guitar is like a beacon of light for hitchhikers. Drivers can see a gig bag sticking up from far away. Plus, people like to support starving musicians.

If I had it to do over, I would ditch the guitar, but put all my clothes in the acoustic gig bag. That way, I could lose the suitcase and still give off good musician vibes. When it's 20 degrees and everything aches, animal instincts take over. By the time I got to Brentwood I was no longer musician, just mammal; evolving in real time, exerting as little effort as possible for maximum gain.

The grueling walk along the highway was over, but all the expensive cars flying by at the exit made my situation look bleak. My thumb was merely a billboard protesting the status quo. Nobody cared. I wasn't allowed on the highway and the BMWs in Brentwood weren't stopping. The drivers didn't even give me eye contact.

**That's when I realized that I had to look for shelter and prepare for a tough night. There were some bushes nearby that looked promising.**

But just before I disappeared from polite society, another cop pulled up, rolled down his window, and asked for my license. He said someone had reported suspicious activity, and asked why I was loitering. I told him my purpose as he ran my ID. "Son, did you know your license is expired?"

"No sir I didn't. I guess it's a good thing I decided to hitchhike." He laughed, which made him sound much more human. "It's a good thing," he agreed. "You know I'm not supposed to do this, but you're not going to catch a ride here. I can take you to the Love's truck stop, about 10 miles south. You'll have better luck down there."

Buzz said you almost never get rides from pretty women, cops, and truckers. I was already two for three and the second anomaly was taking me to the third. "Thank you sir." I said. "That's ten miles closer to where I need to be."

Once we got in, Officer Whitt was even friendlier. He asked about the festival, what type of music I liked to listen to and play. While we were talking, he flipped open his dashboard laptop and put on some background tunes.

"Have you heard Dylan's latest album, Modern Times?"

"No, but a couple months ago, I saw him live in Indianapolis, and he played a few songs from it."

"Cool, I just got it."

As Officer Whitt scrolled through his iTunes library, the patrol car started veering to the left and right.

**I got scared for a minute, until it hit me. In Cop Land, a four-lane highway is really just one big lane. Police don't have any dotted lines.**

Nobody passes them. Officer Whitt wasn't even looking at the road. Then music started playing. The steel guitar slid into my ears and her strings began to cry. We were floating. I didn't even care if Officer Whitt closed his eyes with me. Then his Bobness laid it on us.

"In the still of the night, in the world's ancient light.
Where wisdom grows up in strife.
My bewildered brain, tolls in vain
Through the darkness on the pathways of life."

"When the Deal
Goes Down"

Maybe it was a sign of what modern times will look like one day; vagabonds and cops coexisting in peace.

Officer Whitt dropped me off at Love's around 9:30 pm, wished me luck, and shook my hand as we said goodbye.

I called Melina immediately to tell her that I had just hitched a ride with a huge Dylaphile (or "Bob Cat" as she likes to put it). Mel's the biggest Dylan fan I know; seen dozens of shows. Bob even said hi to her once between songs. I heard it on one of the bootleg recordings. It was sort of unprecedented for him to say anything at all, but sure enough, he stopped the show to make an announcement.

**Ol' Bobby D. said, "I'd like to say hi to the president of our territorial fan club down front, Miss Linda Lou. It looks like someone shuffled her away. I wish she'd come back."**

After hearing this, Melina ran back up to the front and Bob said, "Hey, you're back!"

I told her, "If Bob sweeps you off your feet one day, be sure to ask him if I can tag along. Just give me a small room in the castle. He's got a castle right?"

Melina was just happy I wasn't freezing to death. Her sigh of relief said it all. She finally gave me her blessing.

The temperature was in the mid-teens, so I got right to work: "Hey, I'm playing at a festival in Perdido Key and could really use a ride if you're heading that way." The truckers were all nice, but either they weren't allowed or they weren't going south. I delivered my pitch for a few hours before an older gentleman sounded halfway interested. "I'll think about it," were his exact words. To which I replied, "I'll play for my ride or I'll shut up, either way's cool." The man smiled and said, "I'll be right back." After getting some provisions, he returned. "C'mon, hop in."

**I was three for three in hitchhiker anomalies! Then came the catch. "I gotta warn you though, you'll have to share your seat with another passenger."**

I didn't reply. "What kind of weird kinky trucker shit is this?" I thought. But I was so cold and desperate that I had to scope it out. We walked over to the truck. Dude opened the door and there, sitting on the passenger seat, was the cutest little black poodle I'd ever seen. We both started laughing as my new friend gave me a hearty pat on the back.

His name was Casey Stengel (also the name of a former New York Yankees manager) and then there was Ross, the dog. Casey told me how he'd saved Ross a few years back; said he was backing his truck up when someone shouted "Stop!" Casey got out and found this little pathetic creature lying down next to his tire. Ross was in a state of despair, with long hair like he'd been lost for months, all matted and tangled up with burrs. "It's a good thing I didn't roll over the poor thing. But if I hadn't, he was about to roll over dead. We've been best friends ever since."

Ross sat on my lap the whole way and listened to us talk about life, the universe, and everything. Like me, Casey wanted to be free and see the open country, and trucking accomplished both. He'd been to every state and traveled three million miles with Ross by his side. Since Casey owned his rig, he could turn gigs down and vacation for as long as he wanted after a drop off. As we talked, trucking started to sound less like a redneck stereotype and more like a romantic dream.

**It was heavenly. The entire southern sky looked like fireflies high on cocaine.**

Later on, I found out that it was because the Leonid meteor showers were peaking. There were so many shooting stars that we lost track. Some of them had tails stretching clear across the horizon.

Time flashed by as well. Casey took me all the way to the Love's in Mobile, Alabama, but wouldn't let me go. He insisted on waiting until Buzz arrived to pick me up. As he opened his cooler and started making sandwiches, I got the guitar out and started fingerpicking the riff to my newest song. The least I could do was play for my ride.

"Free Ride Lullaby"

## Free Ride Lullaby

No time to dream American Dreams
Gonna ride the wind and spread my wings
Can't stand the man. Time to run
New vocation vagabond

I adore you babe, but I can't tell
When to kiss and when to bail
I'm so sick and tired of
Broken hearts and chasin' love

I threw away my telephone
Kept my thumb and some rollin' bones
I threw away my piece of pie
For a piece of mind and a battle cry

No time to fear no lookin' back
I found myself on the railroad tracks
I see my breath in the air
Catch a train go anywhere

The Gods are blowin' in my hair
The world is whirlin' I declare
I'm not homeless, I'm home-free
Nothin' nobody can take from me
Free ride lullaby
Free ride

While I played, Casey made me a killer club sandwich. He made a point of saying that he only gets fresh bread and organic produce. I almost felt bad for scarfing it down and not savoring the aged sourdough. While I was shoving food into my face, Casey asked if he could play my guitar.

"Of course!!! Please."

So he picked up my Takamine and started fiddling around. He was pretty rusty, but I could hear the skill buried beneath the years. I could tell that the guitar was once a dear friend. Then finally, Casey remembered the riff and started to sing "Suite: Judy Blue Eyes," by Crosby, Stills and Nash. As he started to sing, Ross started to wag his little tail. Then halfway through the song, this big ol' trucker-of-a man began to cry. He got so choked up that he stopped playing.

"You alright?" I asked.

"Yeah … no, I'm fine," he said. "I just realized … this is the first time I've played for Ross."

I'll never forget their expressions. The little black poodle was looking up at the big burly trucker, listening intently. Apparently, they were having a moment.

It was hard not to keep my composure. Fortunately, Casey also sensed the hilarity and tears turned to laughter. I joined in as Casey picked up the song where he had left off.

It was too much. A flood of emotions washed over me. I began laughing and crying at the same time. I didn't know how to feel because I was feeling so many things at once. At that moment, I suddenly became still.

The closest thing that captures the way I felt comes from the Sanskrit definition of nirvāna. It roughly translates to an "extinction or disappearance"; literally, "a blowing out." That's it. I'm pretty sure I had a blowout. Like a fire that ceases to draw breath and goes out, all my emotions vanished, and for a brief moment there was clarity and gratitude for the gift the universe had given.

When Buzz picked me up, it was still dark. By the time I finished telling my story, we were rolling along the Perdido Key coast as the sun was coming up.

I made good time: sunset to sunrise. But I'll never do it again.

## Arugula
Dec. 11, 2020 | 11 y, 9 mo

The precise moment that I realized Finn would be a writer someday:

Finn: "Arugula. Arugula."

Me: "What?"

Finn: "Arugula. Arugula. Arugula."

Me: "I'm working Dude! What the hell?"

Finn: "Arugulaaaaaa. Isn't it so satisfying?"

## Greyhound grit
May 12, 2013

"Excuse me sir. Where's Beale Street?"

"That-a-way, son [points straight down Second Avenue]."

"Thanks!"

As I walk through old neighborhoods and parks, a few drifters ask for a helping hand. I drop five dollars into a tin can next to an old Black man who's falsetto reminds me of the late Ted Hawkins. As he picks away on his imitation Ovation, I hear a bit of the nimble-fingered Furry Lewis, who I'm sure inspired many a Memphian. Every lick is old and dirty and perfect. He's got a soft voice, a cracked guitar, and a softball-sized lump protruding from his neck. Beale Street can't manufacture his expression. This guy's singin' the blues so he can make it through another day.

Behind us, another man throws peanuts from a window. Then I hear the man's muffled voice say, "Hank's right on time today." A small squirrel comes racing down the sidewalk, crosses the street toward us, avoids the trolley, and starts shelling nuts like a beaver taking down a tree. Chips are flying.

We introduce ourselves. Old man's name is Ed Harris. Harris and Hank have been best buds for a few years now. It looks like Hank is playing a squirrel-sized harmonica as he munches a nut, hunched over like Ed, groovin' to the music and the sounds of the street.

Eddy's got the blues, but he laughs and sings his way through it. As we shoot the shit, he plays several songs while Hank scampers about, sometimes jumping up on Ed's knee to listen.

"Crap! Gotta run!" My Greyhound is about to depart for Nashville. Three hours flew by.

So yeah … If you're searching for something authentic, take the long way to Beale Street. In the bars, you'll hear the same covers played every night and you'll see the same tired look behind the eyes of musicians playing someone else's song. But as old and tired as Ed looks, I'd wager that he's happier than most of those Beale Street cats. Ed follows his own tune, writes his own songs, sings from experience.

You might find him at the corner of Monroe and Main. Stop by and say hi. He may play the same songs that he's played a thousand times, but they'll sound different.

A true bluesman will never play a song the same way twice.

Drop some peanuts on the ground and wait. It shouldn't take long. Hank's right on time.

## Moon switch

Dec. 30, 2020

Once a month, Mel asks me to turn off the outside light and I have to explain that the moon doesn't have a light switch.

But she has many songs to her name. One of my favorites …

"Lady Luna"

## Scraped by an oatmeal

Jan. 31, 2021 | 11 y, 10 mo

Finn: "I got scraped by an oatmeal!"

I thought he was being ridiculous, but sure enough, there was one singular oat sticking up between the stove and the counter he was wiping down. Drew blood and everything.

## Lateral thinking

Feb. 17, 2021 | 11 y, 11 mo

Piled into bed for family time – super cozy. Horizontal never felt better.

Me: "Hey Fiona, can you go upstairs and get the puzzle book?"

Fiona: "You didn't go on a walk with us and get any exercise today."

I knew teaching my kids to make rational arguments would come back to bite me.

## Whataboutism

Mar. 3, 2021

The art of deflection wherein one injustice is purported to be more grave than another.

You've witnessed whatabouters whatabout each other, which is what we call a war of whatabouting.

The one-uppers might as well be cockadoodling 'cause nobody can hear above the shoutabouting.

It's energy sucking.
Such a big kerfuffle
Feathers all ruffled
Gobble gobble gobble
Turkeys squawk and squabble

Every ism's gotta schism.
Every schism has an ism.
Prove me wrong.
And I'll bet you a Benjamin.

You'd think we're all doomed,
that we all got the itis.
We're all inflamed,
every last one of us.

Arthritis
Colitis
Fasciitis

Ask 'em to do the dishes and they'll give you stink-eye-tis.
It's contagious.

Now my little whatabouters have whataboutitis.

## Hacky-sack
May 7, 2021

I bought a hacky sack today because I wanna learn how to be
a cooler nerd.

## Doing the pterodactyl
June 6, 2021

Buster passed away last
night. He never actually
bit anyone. He was a love
pug. Although he almost
gummed my hand off
once when I got between
him and a bone. He was
the runt, so he devoured
his food like his life
depended on it.

Don't ever tell your kids that we don't bite.

Before dinner, he'd let
us know just how long
he'd been waiting. It's hard to describe the noise he made. Finn said
it sounded like a sound that humans never actually heard at all. He
coined the phrase, "Doing the Pterodactyl."

Buster didn't nibble his kibble. His face dove in as he chomped down
to the bottom. The bowl would rattle as it bounced off the floor. If

there wasn't a wall, he would have pushed the bowl into another room trying to get all the little bits that were slimed to the side.

We were all outside reminiscing, telling old Buster and Bobo stories when a little bird hopped across the ground in front of us. She had something white in her beak, but we couldn't quite see what it was. A few of us crouched down to get a closer look. It was a little tuft of fur.

Melina: "It's the circle of life."

Rest in peace Buster. Keep those baby birds warm.

# 12

# Yes, I Really Did **That**

## Beaker goes to Bonnaroo

July 25, 2021

One of my favorite adventures began with an unexpected call from a guy who I had met a few months back. "Wait, who are you? Adam? […] Oh right. The show. Yeah, it was kinda fuzzy." Come to find out, he had just bought a ticket to Bonnaroo but didn't have a car.

I wasn't planning to go to Bonnaroo this summer, let alone in two hours as Adam suggested, but Fate must have a sense of humor, because my colleagues threw a Muppet-themed "Fun Friday" that very day. I had gone to work sporting a white lab coat, googly-eye glasses, a big orange clown nose, orange face paint, and bright orange hair.

Not only did Adam correctly peg me for a festivalgoer, he also happened to catch me on a day when Jim Henson would have rolled in his grave if he found out that Beaker turned down Bonnaroo.

Quick rewind: When we were kids, my sisters, Amber and Willow, used to tease me because I had a high squeaky voice. "Alright, Beaker!

We hear you … shut up!" So when Adam asked if I was going to Bonnaroo, what else could I say but "MEEP MEEP!!!"

Sisters Willow and Amber

For those of you who don't speak Beakonese, that translates to "HELL YEAH!!!"

Even Mrs. Beaker agreed that the Universe had spoken, so I stuffed a few essentials into my oversized lab coat pockets (small spray bottle, Scotch tape, a pocket knife) and took off.

It was about an hour drive before we rolled into Manchester. I couldn't go to the main gate because I didn't have a ticket, so we turned into a driveway nearby. As we pulled up, an older couple – retired maybe – greeted us from their rocking chairs on the porch where they were enjoying the sunset. They looked like nice country folks. Adam waved hello as I rolled down my window and greeted the neighbors.

"Meep Meep!"

It took a second, but the old feller squinted hard, then rocked his head back and exploded. He wheezed hard as he exhaled; a laugh that sounded as funny as my stupid face looked.

After we all regained composure, Adam jumped in. "What my friend was trying to say, is that we're looking for a place to park for a few days." The old man didn't hesitate. "Absolutely! Right over there would be fine." The neighbors were charging 30 bucks per day, but when I asked if we could pony up, the man wouldn't have it. "Oh stop. What good is your Muppet money?"

At that point, we split up. Adam headed for the entrance, and Beaker for the back door. Festival staff were everywhere, driving around in golf carts, on patrol for idiots like me. The bright white lab coat and orange hair didn't make for the greatest camo, so I was ducking for cover, dashing from ditch to ditch, avoiding flashlight beams.

Thankfully, there was a farm up ahead where I took refuge. I trekked through a couple of fields before entering a wooded area with big evergreens blocking out the Bonnaroo lights. Suddenly, a loud "RRRRIBIT!!!" stopped me dead in my tracks.

"Hmm ... bullfrogs usually live by water." At that moment, my eyes adjusted to the night and I realized that my next step would have landed my ass off a ledge into a slimy pond. I would have sludged back to the car and driven home in shame if it had not been for my little green guardian.

It was a good omen. So I walked around the pond, through the woods, right into the campground I'd been aiming for.

"Aces."

After a few phone calls, I got a hold of some friends. They had a giant lifesize Batman figure on top of their camper, so it was easy to find. These guys were die-hard fans, part of the InfoRoo community, the festival's online forum where people discuss pro tips, afterparties, and where to find … how do I put it? … fun ways to feel smarter and better looking than they really are.

My friends were all flipping out over me showing up on a whim as Beaker. We hung out for a bit, but I was eager to see Ice Cube. He was about to go on, and there was still the business of breaking into the festival grounds.

The festival wall was too tall to climb, so I took off and walked around the perimeter looking for ideas. Then I saw her, yet another friend, growing in the perfect spot. But her lowest limb was about 12 feet off the ground. So I turned sideways and shimmied up between the fortress wall and the trunk of the old oak, until I could wrap my hands around a branch and hoist myself up. From there, it was an easy climb over the fence where I dropped down.

Once on my feet, I saw giant excavators and bulldozers everywhere.

Beaker: "MEEP!!!"

Bulldozer: "Hey! Watch your mouth."

Beaker: "Uh-oh!"

Someone from InfoRoo had spiked the punch. It was probably Batman. He doesn't have any real superpowers. Probably came to Bonnaroo to score some performance enhancers. No wonder he thinks he can fly.

After weaving around a maze of machinery, I came to another fence with a long line of campers on the other side. It was chain linked, so I could easily climb up and over. Or so I thought. About five feet up, the whole thing caved forward into the side of an RV. If not for the music blasting inside, I'm sure the occupants would have spilled out to see what the bump was about.

So there I was, teetering atop one wibbly-wobbly fence, leaning against an RV, trying not to get my nuts sliced off, grasping around in the dark for a way to regain balance. Luckily, an air conditioner jutting out provided enough leverage to lift myself up and over the fence.

Now I was in. Across the field, I saw someone playing onstage. I was so excited that I broke character and shouted "Wahooooo!" But my elation quickly faded as my near-vision kicked in and I realized just how many people were staring at me. I wasn't anywhere near the stage but had barged into the middle of a raging party. Open bar, everybody dressed to the nines … a little too fancy for the occasion. One super-tall dude with jet black hair looked familiar.

**"Is that Jack White?" I thought. "It can't be. OH SHIT!"**

I had just stumbled into Bonnaroo's open-air Green Room where all the artists were getting drunk and schmoozing with celebrity guests. I knew the campground looked entirely too posh. There were far too many feather boas concentrated in one place for these to be normal people. And then there was Beaker, looking as dazed and confused as he would on The Muppet Show after blowing up the lab.

White was looking at me like I was a circus monkey that needed to get on with the act, like an Oompa Loompa who needed to sing his little jig, then disappear through a hidden door. He had my sympathy. I was seeing all kinds of strange and colorful things myself but could not find any crack in space or time through which to escape. My presence was starting to get awkward for the people in feather boas. I was either paid entertainment or a crazy person.

Suddenly, a figure in black appeared. "Sir?" the man inquired (which I thought was rather gratuitous, considering who I was), "Can I please see your wristband?" Rolling up my sleeve was clearly not an option, so I decided to reciprocate with politeness: "No, thank you. I'm good." The guy didn't expect that one. "Stay here. I'm getting my supervisor."

In a last-ditch effort, I put my hand on the gentleman's shoulder, leaned in close, and looked directly into his eyes. "Just let me go back to where I came from," I suggested persuasively, in a low soothing tone. To my surprise, he obligingly repeated, "Just go back to where you came from."

**I totally Obi-Wan Kenobi'd the man in black. I was a golden god! … or copper-faced Muppet on acid. The two are virtually indistinguishable.**

Armed with this knowledge, I turned and disappeared whence I came. Only I wasn't about to climb the wibbly-wobbly fence again, so I skirted along the line of campers, stopping occasionally to listen to the music inside. I had recognized an Avett Brothers song earlier when I crashed into the camper, but realized now that it was the Avett Brothers. They were rehearsing.

Finally, I found the exit to the VIP camp which connected to the main festival grounds. As I beelined through, I put my hand on the bouncer's arm and said, "I'll be back," reassuringly, pointing to his eyes and then to mine as I gave the googly eye glasses a little jiggle. He inaudibly mouthed "What the fuck?"

I never returned, but I wanted him to remember me so I could get back in. Like right before the festival ended, it would have been a fun place to get kicked out … for real.

**I must have been the whitest orange person pounding my fist to '90s gangsta rap. It was totally surreal.**

Thirty thousand protesters shouting, in unison, "Fuck tha police!" No one demanded to frisk me. Nobody asked for my wristband either; the lab coat covered the spot where it should have been.

The rest of the night was wild, a blur, like an impressionist landscape painted with fluorescent watercolors. My canvas was alive, with every person enveloped in a warm glow. I don't remember all the details, but the feelings are ingrained into my subconscious. The freedom to live large in your own little way is a legacy that I hope to pass on.

The next day, I woke up on a blow-up couch, staring up at Batman. He gave me a wink and reassured me that I had made it home safely to the InfoRoo tent. After breakfast and lots of laughter, I took my leave and headed to the campground exit to look for wristbands.

Sure enough, someone forgot to wear sunscreen the day before and was burnt out. The car was fully packed and the driver did not look happy.

I waved him over and asked nicely, "Hey, mind giving me your wristband if you're not coming back?" The guy said, "Sure" and let me cut the wristband off with my pocket knife. "I'm just glad someone can use it." I told him his contribution would not go to waste, that we were kin – me from the orange, and he from the red-faced clan.

The Scotch tape in my lab coat pocket came in handy as I put the band back together. This was far from my first rodeo. During my college years, when I was broke, I had perfected the art of sneaking into Bonnaroo. One time, I literally walked backward through the exit, which consisted of a giant arch with a constant flood of people passing through … in one direction. Every time a staff member looked at me, I started walking forward like I was walking with the crowd. As soon as they looked away, I put myself back in reverse until my ass was in. I got ten bucks for winning that bet.

**A few years later, in 2010, the lead singer of GWAR singled me out in the audience with his big black alien penis cannon.**

Shortly before production staff rolled the prop out, the crowd had opened up a large circle for me to swirl my Tree of Life tapestry. As I flew by, my cape created a powerful fanning effect that cooled the surrounding crowd. Becoming a Breeze 101. (We'll come back to that.)

So when the singer for GWAR saw me prancing around out in the open, he turned the cannon and blasted me with a stream of alien penis blood. I mean, it was dark red, so that's what I'm going with. I'd hate to think I was getting peed on.

Meanwhile, the circle that opened up for me was expanding, to the point that I remember seeing the mosh pit come into view at one end. Shortly after this realization (or warning), out of nowhere, someone ran up from behind and spearheaded me in the back, tackling me to the ground. The spot on my spine where his head hit should have hurt, but the adrenaline was masking the pain.

Clearly, someone thought I was having too much fun and wanted to steal the show. I was slow getting up. People were closing in to fill the space. My circle was coming to an end! The idea of a circle ending crossed my mind and didn't even sound possible. The rat bastard broke my fucking circle! Then I turned around to find, not a rat, but a bro twice my size, staring down at me, looking more like a bull. And not the sweet flower-sniffer type like Ferdinand.

I wanted to be pissed off, but the giant didn't give me a choice. I knew the only way to beat Muscles was in a meeting of the mind. So I pretended to be a Spanish matador and moved gracefully around the collapsing circle as I twirled my cape, taunting the beast to join me in a dance of death. Surprisingly, he caught on and made horns with his fingers above his forehead. Fully transformed, he started kicking the dirt back with his "hooves," signaling that a charge was imminent.

"Let's dance, bitch!"

So we did this whole routine where he chased me down and ran through my cape. All the while a giant stream of alien penis blood was raining down upon us. It was metal as fuck. The circle opened back up, but now people had their phones out taking videos.

I'm pretty sure GWAR kept the song going just for us, but at some point, we must have drained that alien penis dry. The band repeated the hook during the final refrain and it all came to an end. This was it. As the bull passed through one last time, my foot was strategically planted just out of sight behind the cape. As the beast ducked under my arms, he tripped and fell forward. There wasn't enough time to get his hands down off his head, but thankfully for him, his face was there to soften the blow.

"Splat!" … right into a puddle of mud.

The bull got up on all fours. His face besmirched, completely caked in alien penis blood. Me, I was satisfied, but failed to plan for anything past revenge, let alone the possibility of being gored to death. I should have been dribbling in my pants, but I was still high enough to think it was hilarious.

Dude jumped to his feet and lurched forward. I jumped back, but he had already grabbed a hold of my hand. I wasn't expecting what came next. With a firm grasp, he simply wiggled my limp arm up and down as if to say, "We're even." The gentle beast then pulled me in and gave me two "Well played!" pats on the back before disappearing into the pit to batter someone else's brains. I was flabbergasted. It was a Bonnaroo miracle. Turns out the big softy had a little Ferdinand in him after all.

After the show, I had groupies who followed me around from one party to the next. I also had a bone bruise on my spine that stuck with me for about five months. One thing's for sure, I was not built for the pit, but I do like to be front and center.

Which brings us to my last magic trick. If you want to rock out next to the band without having to camp out by the stage for hours, bring a spray bottle full of ice water. The next part is simple: Just spray your way to the front. Moses would have been proud, for a mere Muppet parted a great sea of sweaty men and glistening women. Only, this was no miracle. It was just homeostasis. Hot hippies + cool water = equilibrium.

One lady signaled for more and revealed a few places that needed an extra squirt. She was super hot and needed extra cooling, so I sprayed her entire body down. I didn't mind the detour (for science, of course). There was lots of homeostasis happening as I parted the Partying Sea.

The crowd practically rolled out the red carpet as I misted my way through. I wasn't cutting; it was an unspoken understanding. They moaned in ecstasy as I breezed by. I gave them a nod that shook my googly eyes and they giggled from the gut. It was a good deal all around.

This completes Becoming a Breeze 101 for today. Your homework: Take a picture of the band, up close, no zooming. If it's pixelated you get an F.

The pit is where you'll find my people. We're a little crazy-looking, or looking for fun, rather. We're lovers of loud music. It's gotta jiggle your innards. You'll find us swaying together in solidarity. When the sound is especially exhilarating, you might catch us acknowledging the glory by looking directly at each other … eye to googly eye.

## SpongeBob blow job

Sept. 9, 2021

Counting the infinite solar systems and parallel universes, I don't think anyone will ever utter these words in this order: SpongeBob broke my neck giving me a blow job today.

True story.

It was cool at first, just a little light toe licking, but then it got weird.

Joking aside, this actually originated from an old sand volleyball injury. I thought it was all healed up, but not so much. My C-5 bulging disc hates me and my headstand here. It was totally worth getting the trick shot though. Definitely the coolest boxkite I've ever seen.

## Dimensions of Truth
Sept. 20, 2021

Truth is found in shades of grey
between black and white lies a doorway
where in walks Yang, out walks Yin
They work hard, but take it easy and sing
for love, for hate? Is it art or graffiti?
Is it all fake or is it Armine?
Who cares? It's a bag ... floating in the air
It's American beauty, a billionaire
who took all the money and gave it away
A swan song on his dying day
An echo that bounces eternally
in the swirl of a Fibonacci
sequence.

We live forever
in the things we create,
in every endeavor
we offend the Fates

Heaven on earth is a legacy
It's living electromagnetically
Positive, negative; a time for each way
for a three-dimensional shade of grey

## Colors
Sept. 15, 2021

Blue like the sky
Looks good in the rain
Whenever she's grey
Her tears float away
Never to complain

Brown's down and dirty
Smells like the rain
Alchemy petrichor
Mother Earth troubadour
Tokin' Mary Jane

Green so full of life
A waltz in the rain
Bring on the flood
She's ready to bud
In the middle of a hurricane

Purple is a witch
No end to her reign
Don't ever oppose her
I'm a lizard chauffeur
Flying her purple plane

Pink don't give a damn
Naked in the rain
California
Loves you … phoria
Likes the smell of cocaine

Orange is an artist
Holds her own reins
I tried to figure Orange out
She's a door hinge
on a roundabout

Red pistol passion
Paris in the rain
Sips her liquor
Lips a trigger
Sweet as sugarcane

Yellow burns the Sun
for his lover, Miss Rain
The love they seek
is bittersweet
Rainbows die in vain

## Water flosser

Oct. 5, 2021 | 12 y, 7 mo

Getting ready for the day.

Finn: "What is a water flosser?"

Me: "Oh this here? It shoots a high-pressured stream of water into the cracks between your teeth.

Finn: So it's a bidet for your teeth?"

Me: "Yes."

Finn: "I'm sold."

"I guess the tree don't grow very far from the apple" – Stephen Wilson Jr.

"I guess the tree don't grow very far from the apple" – Stephen Wilson Jr.

# How to get yourself murdered

Oct. 6, 2021

It's my first time seeing Ani DiFranco, and I'm instantly hypnotized. She's a ferocious little chipmunk. Guitar strings rattle and pop as she scampers across the stage – totally in love with life.

I'm so lost in her spell that I barely notice my wife slip away to get a drink. A few minutes later Melina returns, standing where she was, in front and a little to the left.

I start scratching her back along with some light massaging. This goes on for a couple minutes until the end of the song – when a large Black lady turns around. She's an orbulant beauty.

(Orbulant /OR-byuh-lent/: adjective. 1. Round, radiant. 2. Not in the dictionary. 3. Looks nothing like Melina.)

"HELLO?!" snaps the stranger in front of me.

I literally levitate off the ground, then cover my face. I try to explain what happened, but I'm laughing so hard that it doesn't make sense. Apparently, her husband had gone off to get a drink too, so she thought I was him the whole time.

Then her husband walks up. He looks like Mr. Clean, but with prison-yard tattoos coiling over every bulging muscle. Suddenly the tats start to shape-shift and expand. Nobody spiked my drink. The guy was just flexing. As he towers over me, I pray that he's merely big-bear-hug scary and not "Hulk smash!" scary.

Hulk: "Dude, did you just touch my wife?!"

Fight or flight mode kicks in. However, instead of running, I decide to tell a joke instead – see where it goes.

I blurt: "Yeah, I was scratching her back because I thought she was my wife. Look, my wife is walking up now. She can scratch your back if you want and we can call it even. I'm sure she won't mind."

He laughs, which is my face's cue to turn from pale-white ghost back to pink-white ginger. We all laugh.

What a testament to Ani DiFranco's talent – that she could entrance two strangers into sharing such an intimate moment, completely unaware of each other's name, face, or race. Music will always be colorblind like that. And I'll always be an idiot.

I then do an about-face and power walk to the farthest corner of the club, where I can properly short-circuit in private. I'm still in shock, wiping tears between waves of laughter.

Melina walks up, wearing a familiar look of confusion, but I can only say three words before bursting out into a high-pitched giggle. I sound like a mad scientist but more ridiculous, like Beaker. "I just scratched …" is all I can get out.

Later on, we pass the couple and I give Mel a little scratch on the back. They laugh, again. But it's different this time. I know what mockery looks like. Their eyebrows squinch a bit.

I lower my head, but refuse to surrender.

"Hey, y'all know where to find me if you get an itch."

## Bathroom rave
Dec. 19, 2021

It irks me no end when public bathrooms install auto faucets but go half-ass with the manual soap dispensers. I like to get my hands wet first. And of course the faucet gets me thinking that the soap dispenser is also automatic, but when you wave your hands around to get soap, nothing happens.

Before long, you look like you're at a rave, waving your hands around like an idiot. Meanwhile, some dude walks over, gets the soap, and looks at me like I'm a monkey that's still figuring out how to use tools as I hit the side of the dispenser, grunting out of confusion. It's either that or he whispers, "Hey dude, how much for whatever you're on?"

## Food poisoning

Jan. 17, 2022

Ate some bad salsa last night. Felt the yuck coming on real strong, so I ate a frozen crushed ginger cube with honey, took a Tummy Soother, drank five big cups of water and 15 minutes later I was playing Codenames again. All good, except I might have offended Piper. She doesn't like it when I'm farty. Which is ironic for a creature that rolls in the yuck. Sometimes she woofs at me if she's in the line of fire. No joke. I have to go to another room for the damn dog.

## A laugh that'll live forever

Feb. 11, 2022

Pat Metheny blew us away last night. Pretty sure he's the best guitarist I've seen. I've said that a time or two before, after seeing Phil Keaggy, but Metheny is on a whole different level. Or rather, he's not level. He's a whirling riptide vortex that sucks you in and spits you out. But it's a fun ride, so you're just glad that you made it out alive to tell the story.

Metheny is a mad scientist. He actually sequenced robotic arms to play the vibes, xylophones, and several other percussive instruments. I'm still trying to figure out how to describe his sound. Planet formation, maybe? In any case, brilliant syncopation and genre-bending orchestrations.

The piano man had four keyboards, a B3 organ and played the baby grand like a dream. His midi controller was a standup bass that rattled when he hammered the keys down. Drummer was old school New Orleans at its peak.

Pat had a guitar with three harps built in. There were strings stacked on strings stacked on strings that he played with two hands, like a piano.

"Beautiful" doesn't capture it. Maybe if I went full on Tourette's and randomly whispered expletives, that might capture the raw emotion. "Whispered" because the crowd was so quiet you could hear a pin drop.

At one point, Pat was playing solo on his harp guitar while the robots were taking five. Melina was coming back from the bathroom, when during an especially quiet moment of a masterpiece, she booted a beer can across the aisle. The space was finely tuned for acoustics, so as the can skipped and crashed against the seats, every little clang could be heard throughout the performance hall. Then, as she passed by her brother, Melina kicked the stupid thing again. "Why is that here?" she asked the universe. The universe responded with laughter from everyone in the balcony audience.

At this point, the can was spinning under someone's seat, still making noise. It was a metallic whirl of a sound, as if someone was playing the can like a flute. Turns out, it was spinning under Melina's seat, because upon sitting down, she managed to kick that damn can a third time.

I buried my head in my hands. Melina crashed into my shoulder so her face could take refuge from all the shame coming from Balcony 1.

Then I saw the can next to my feet and did what had to be done.

"Crunch!"

We were seated at the bottom of the balcony, dead center. Both sets of speakers were pointed right at us, so they were the best seats in the house for sound. Also the perfect place to kick a can three times. Everyone above us got a nice view.

The Melster giggled for the duration of the song. Random outbursts of laughter continued throughout the show, and even later on in bed, which sorta killed the mood. It would be cooler if I was talking about sex, but we were just trying to sleep.

And just like the can with nine lives, this story continues to make noise … in your laughter as you read these lines. Who knows, maybe it's a laugh that'll live forever.

# Love Is

March 23, 2022

Happy Anniversary Melina! Eleven years, baby! Remember our second anniversary, when that stupid comedian at The Basement called us out from the stage and gave us "two years, tops." I knew we'd be together forever because I really wanted to spite him … I mean, because I love you.

Way to prove Douchebag wrong. Your spite is strong. Rhyme intended, which is a nice segue into the poem I wrote for you:

### Love Is

Love is a cage with a key
Stuck together. Forever free

Love is pain when one's away
When two hearts separate

Love is learning how to fight
Makin' up with neck bites

Love is fireworks and confetti
We blow up, but float down steadily

Love is when body's meet
When heads won't, but hearts beat … together

Love is when the kids are seven
Making the radio go to eleven

Love is a lotta strange sounds
Makes 'em feel safe and bound … together

Love is music, casting spells
We cast 'em right on ourselves

Love is a cage with a key
Stuck together. Forever free

# Call me Al

July 2, 2022

The only thing I know is that I don't know anything, but I don't know that for sure. Because maybe there are some things that I do actually know. But I'll never know the things that I know, unless I die and God tells me, "Hey dude, you almost had it right back there, but here's where you fucked up." God cusses. I'm pretty sure. And I hope God is up there ... or down here somewhere ... so he or she can tell my wife that I was right all along.

God: "Yes, Darby, the airspeed velocity of an unladen swallow is 20.1 miles per hour. Well done, my good and faithful servant."

Me: "I wasn't that faithful. I'm sorry."

God: "Right again. That's just something we say."

Me: "Just curious. Do you cuss?"

God: "Of course."

Me: "Are you really God?"

God: "Hahaha ... no."

Me: "What!? Then who are you?"

God: "Santa Claus."

Me: "Really?"

God: "Fuck no! I'm God, but call me Al.

Me: "Al? Ohhhh, right. Allah. Hold on, that wasn't a lie back there was it?"

Al: "No. It was a joke. I'm allowed to joke."

Me: "I knew it!"

*Note:* I totally stole a bit from Chris and Jack to make "Call me Al" work. Watch their short sketch, "The White Room," to see which one and we'll call it even. I love those guys – so funny!

"The White Room"

## Hey Google

Oct. 18, 2022 | 13 y, 7 mo

Eating dinner.

Mel: "Hey Google. Do Siamese twins share the same heart?"

Google: "Some people ask if Siamese twins can be born vaginally. Would you like to know more about Siamese twins born vaginally?"

Mel & Finn: "NO!!!"

Me: "Hahaha!"

Finn: "What?"

Me: "I thought it was funny because it sounded like Google said 'born veginally.'"

Finn: "I thought she said 'vaginally.'"

Me: "She did, but it sounded like 'veginally' in her Aussie accent.

Fiona: "Hahahaha!"

Throughout dinner, random bursts of laughter interrupted conversation. No one dared to ask why.

## Dark space

Nov. 30, 2022

Our dog recently taught our cat how to pull open the back screen door. It's impressive. Requires some pretty swift paw-to-nose coordination. So now Xena applies her new skill to kitchen cabinets in search of a little nibble. And when I reach into a dark space to grab my toolbox, it's not surprising at all to have a black cat jump out. I about shat myself. So now I knock on the door to see if my little warrior princess is home before I go barging into her dark space.

## Christmas wishes

Dec. 26, 2022

Now that it's over, go on, relax.
Forget the shopping, all the maniacs.

Eat, drink and be thankful you can.
Stay up late, call a friend.
Take care of your health.
Love and live large.
Learn something new.
Pick up a guitar.

Give something to someone.
Karma will pay,
or maybe it won't,
but it makes the day
brighter.

And maybe that extra energy
adds to the collective memory
which plays over and over in dreams,
whispers, "You're worthy."
A color scheme
is all we are,
we're mixed up and tainted.

Bob Ross would say,
"No, you're just painted!"
Christmas lights.
Toys galore.
Some have none.
Some have more.

Take a breath.
Ahhhhhhhhh
Go on and breathe.
Mama ain't buying no diamond ring.
You gotta earn it!
And as soon as you do,
let it go. Let it be.
Let it pass through
to the next life.

No arrogant ego,
you can have some pride.
Be proud of a life
that learns to die.

Merry Christmas!

## Suki Da

Dec. 26, 2022

One day, my mother-in-law's pug couldn't wait for dinner, so she helped herself to some mushrooms in the backyard. Now, a hound dog like mine comes from a canine line evolved for olfactory work. With her giant schnoz, Piper can smell every dinner in the neighborhood, even reverse-engineer the recipes from a whiff o' shit.

**Unfortunately, for Suki, a pug's mug was bred to make people laugh when they see it. Her nose can't pick out the poison from your yard-variety mushroom like Piper's can.**

So when Suki puked in the kitchen, I didn't think much of it. Some of us figured she got a few too many scraps. We ended up putting Suki in her carrying case to keep her from begging.

After the feast, Fiona released the mini mastiff. Suki was so excited, she got the zoomies and raced around the house. Except she didn't make it around the first lap. She rounded the first bend and plowed straight into the wall. Thankfully, pugs are good at smashing into things with their face. How do you think they got to looking that way?

I was horrified when I saw her, until I realized that was just how she looked all the time. But within 10 minutes, she got worse: wobbling to and fro, nosediving for the toy she was trying to pick up. It was then that the penny dropped and I recalled seeing brown rubbery bits in her puke. Yaya immediately took Suki to the animal hospital.

We were all terrified. Sure enough, the labs came back and confirmed our suspicion. They were shrooms. Fortunately for our little court jester, she was only tripping balls. The vet said she'd be fine in a few hours, after the, "flying purple elephants disappeared" – exact words.

Melina told me to go say something to make her mother feel better about everything, so I walked her and Suki out to the car.

"G'night Jane! Sorry for not telling you Suki puked right away. You had worked so hard making dinner. I just wanted to clean it up without you worrying about another mess."

I couldn't get the joke I had rehearsed in my head out. I was afraid to say it in front of my mother-in-law, but Jane must have read my mind, because it's word-for-word what came out of her mouth.

**"Maybe we should get Suki to show us where those magic mushrooms are!"**

We both laughed. "That's what Lisa said," she added. Jane had just hung up the phone with Lisa, her best friend, fellow nurse and soldier in war (i.e. Duke's ICU). Jane retired from 40 years of service there, and Lisa can't wait to retire in a year, so she can go on long walks in the woods with Suki.

"I don't know," I replied. "I don't think I can trust that schnoz of hers."

Jane laughed even harder as she pulled away with her crazy dog.

Correction: None of us call her a "dog" anymore. We call her " Suki Da," which is much more fitting for an enlightened being.

# 13

# My **Privilege**

## White privilege at Black Poetry night

April 28, 2023

Yesterday, I took my dad to what we thought was a songwriter night, but after we signed up at the front desk, we walked in to find ourselves in the middle of a Black poetry night. The open mic was open to all, but there was only one white chick who showed up after us. She was a regular who ended up reading a silly piece about hockey, one of the whitest sports there is — right behind curling.

**This place was black. DJ was spinning. Nails were glowing under the black lights. Diverse ages, young and old. The smell of fish frying and potatoes stewing was all the menu anyone needed.**

The place was poppin'. And then there was me and my old man, dressed like cowboys with acoustic guitars, like a Hallmark movie that got lost and wandered into a twerk circle that needed baptism.

I found out about this so-called songwriter night through Meetup. com's Raleigh Songwriter club. I assumed that the one and only event they advertised would be for, you know, songwriters. But whatever. We were there, the place was chill, people were cool. We rolled with it. Plus, the MC said we could do whatever the fuck we wanted. Dangerous words for men raised on tractor fumes and mild concussions.

*"Whatever the fuck"* must have been the theme. It was raw, ugly, beautiful. It was bad and wrong done right. One guy shouted, "The only period that's ever stopped me was at the end of a sentence." The crowd shouted "Rewind!" which meant Dude had to repeat himself while everyone snapped their fingers and laughed their asses off.

Despite the animated laughter, everyone had mad respect. Nobody talked over the poet. It reminded me of the Bluebird Cafe in Nashville, where you literally get shushed out the door for being too loud. This place was an anomaly. Most open mics are awful. You're lucky to have a handful of friends listen while the rest of the bar yaks over your art.

Last night, there must have been 80 people glued to the stage, hanging on every word. If it hadn't rained so hard that evening, the place would have been packed.

"Alright, we've got some fresh meat tonight. Coming all the way from Tennessee, my Nashville brother, give it up for Mr. Darby."

Everyone was super warm — cheers were welcoming.

"Thank you! So when my son was itty-bitty, about 1 year old, he woke up one day with some seepage around his eye, like this crud had dried up and completely glued his eyelids shut. It was gross. So being the weirdo that I am, it inspired me to write my first rap ... which goes:

> Boogies in ya nose, crust in ya eye
> Working on a poo makes you cry.
> Cry for ya suppah. Cry for ya sleep
> You don't know numbers so ya can't count sheep!!!"

I got a few laughs, some snappy fingers. I was sooooo white.

"I know we're only supposed to do one piece, but that was just an introduction to my second rap song that I wrote a few weeks back.

The crowd shouted "New shit!" which is a little call and response they do. The MC told me you have to tell the crowd if it's new shit or old shit.

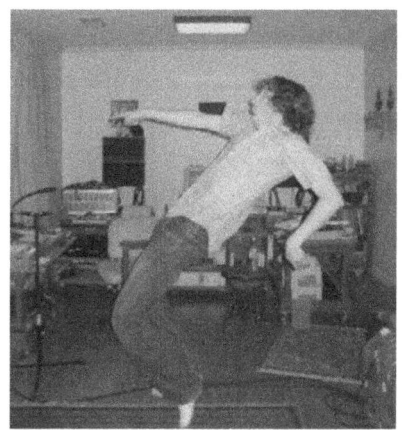

"Yeah, this one is brand new. I wrote it on the road, hopped up on Adderall, driving 10 hours to Cincinnati to pick up my dad and move him here to Raleigh. So this is our home now!"

Everyone cheered.

"And this is the whitest rap you'll ever hear … called 'Fat Baby Legs.'

> Chunky chunky chunk … fat baby legs
> Chicka chicka boom … chicka lay that egg
> Pretty pretty please … don't make me beg
>
> A little Darb'll do, but easy on the nutmeg
> Talkin' talkin' talkin' stop talkin' just dance
> Party party party gotta gimme romance
> Shake-a shake-a shake … ice in the glass
> Billy Goat outta nowhere chewing on my pants
>
> Love gotta beat like a bongo drum
> Boom baby boom baby … apple bottom bum
> Chop choppa chop … Hellacoppa chopping
> Watchin' through the window … I'm naked in an apron
>
> Slather peanut butter peanut butter jelly
> Lick a lick a lick … it off of her belly
> But she didn't shave her hair … got real scruffy
> Fuzzy wuz a bear but Fuzzy wasn't fuzzy
>
> So I gave her the slip … got an upgrade
> Gotta new girl … she my mama marmalade
> Shot shot shot … spike the lemonade

I lay a lay a lay ... her down in the shade
Dip a dip a dip, I dip ya in some fondue
Tricky tricky treat ... I take a trick or two
Yippity skippity whoopty fuckin' do
What the fox say? I don't care. Cow go moo!
Love a love a love ... love her warts and all
One time she let it rip ... killed a fly on da wall
1 2 3 4 5 6 7 8 ... Ride a bull
I'm a Stallion she donkey ... we be makin mule

Rock it rock it rock it ... shake ya head bang bang
Stomp stomp stomp ... freakin' out the dog mang
Change in ya pocket shakin' like a piggy bank
Back 'at ass up baby like boomerang

She a strong-willed woman, like Wilma Flintstone
She ride a motorcycle, gotta mind of her own
My baby like to blow you know she blow a trombone
And boogie when the Bengals are in the end zone

Rub a dub dub in my tub bubble bath
My baby so hot, she broke a thermostat
We be gettin' biblical, kids we begat
Fat baby legs. They feet go pitter pat

Chunky chunky chunk ... fat baby legs
Chicka chicka boom ... chicka lay that egg
Pretty pretty please ... don't make me beg
A little Darb'll do ya, easy on the nutmeg

Thank you."

The whole joint lit up and the DJ started spinning to keep the energy going. They thought Cowboy was gonna sing a little ditty, which is what I thought I'd do too, but you know ... when in Rome.

Later on, I went outside to shoot the shit with everyone hanging out by the food. We were all laughing and carrying on when this lady, out of nowhere, had to make it weird.

She be like, "So what do you think about your privilege?"

"Awww Jeez. What do I think? Damn ... I don't know. I guess it feels pretty good."

Dude sitting next to the lady about chokes on a biscuit and coughs it up while laughing his ass off at the same time. Chic looks pissed off.

"It feels pretty good, does it?"

"Well, yeah. I didn't say I earned it, but ..."

"He said it feels pretty good!"

"A lot of it is luck of the draw."

"Luck of the draw my ass. I work my ass off and you're gonna say it's luck of the draw?"

Dude's still laughing and says, "Chill out. That's the first time I heard that one. He's just telling the truth hahahaha."

I agreed. "You don't choose the hand you're dealt. You choose how to play it. That's you working your ass off."

So I turned and walked away cause she needed to cool off. Inside, the DJ was spinning, music was bumping. My dad and I were talking to these two young ladies on the couch next to us. The MC was trying to get everyone up, so his sister started pulling people out of their seats. Now everyone was dancing except these two stiff looking cowboys. One lady noticed and was like, "uh-uhhh, nope." So she came over and tried to beckon my dad up. MC started chanting, "Go Steve. Go Steve." But his knees have been so bad lately that I knew he'd hurt himself. I jumped up and saved his ass by getting right up behind hers, but facing away.

As soon as our piggy banks touched, she began to shake until she about broke my bank.

The whole bar noticed and began to close in on us. Then into the circle walked a beautiful young lady who decided she was going to be the other piece of bread. So there I was, squished up between two fine looking ladies. My arms were doing the airplane cause the rest of me couldn't really move. They had me sandwiched in while everyone around was going nuts to the music.

After the song ended, I leaned into the lady who I had just pissed off moments earlier, and said, "It was my great privilege to have danced with you." She squinted her eyes, which betrayed the smile that was forming. She didn't want to admit that I was right. I was privileged. And she did feel pretty good. Feels good when people do nice things to you that you don't deserve. She didn't have to apologize. She just kissed me on the cheek, turned, and walked away.

## Be prepared
Jan. 14, 2023

I think it is a good idea to be prepared. This is why I always carry a banana in my pocket. Just in case.

## Taco Tuesday
Jan. 27, 2023

I really thought I was gonna chuck up some tacos last night. Must have been the sprouts hiding in the salad. It was soooo bad. Felt like aliens probing me from the inside. Sounded like they were gurgling guacamole.

Thankfully, just before becoming immobile, I popped four Tummy Soothers and crashed on the couch. Any movement was a bad choice. Felt like Jesus giving my intestines an Indian burn for not blessing the meal.

Fifteen minutes later, the Soothers did their thing and I was farting the poison out like a champ. Everybody hated me, including the dog, who ran out of the room, but I felt like a million bucks.

This concludes my PSA on Tummy Soothers. Do it.

## Smoke

Jan. 29, 2023

```
    /
   )(
  ( / )
  ( ) \ )
```
Smoke
blows left
It blows right
Goes with the force
that blows your kite
Smoke blows forward
Sometimes it blows behind
You might lose a good thing
that you have to go back and find
Eventually your fire burns right out
You're stuck in whatever you're in
Digging down for burning embers
just waiting for the winds again
Sometimes when it gets dark
Everything's completely still
Smoke floats straight up
Goes all the way up until
It dissipates into wind
Becomes the force
that's blowin'
smoke
```
  ( \ ( )
  ( /)(
  )(
  /
```

## My dream

March 23, 2023

Someday I'll be told
I attended your wedding
A boy growin' old
Forgetting I'm forgetting

You'll forget that I forgot your name
Smile when I look sad
But I'll look at you the same
Just as I always had

I'll still beam with pride
When my mind fades away
To have you by my side
Like the autumn day
When I first saw your face
The moon was filled with envy
So I put him in his place
And made us a memory
That I'll keep until it's gone
I'm sorry to say it this way
But love will pass on
In our grandchildren's play

And I don't know for sure
But wishful nonetheless
That life will endure
And souls will transgress
Beyond this ball of dirt
Where the moon will take a pass
As he chases your skirt
You'll step on the gas
Burn by, blow up, explode
Becoming everything

Let us then grow old
So I can die for you my Dream

Love, Scoob

130

# Excommunication

June 9, 2023 | 14 y, 3 mo

We're on a tour of Athens, in an ancient Greek Orthodox Church, hundreds of years old, gold-leaf iconography everywhere. Trying to get one good picture for Nana.

Me: "Smile ..."

Finn and Fiona: [Blank stares.]

Me: "... a little less like you live in a concentration camp."

They hold their stoic stares while the guy next to us starts to chuckle, which turns into a bad case of the giggles. People are lighting candles around us. Dude starts laughing so hard that he has to excommunicate himself from the church. As he runs for the door, the teenagers finally crack a smile.

Me: "Got it!"

## Athenian drivers are craaaaaazy!

June 14, 2023

Driving in downtown Athens is like riding a tricycle through NYC during rush hour.

At least I didn't see anyone looking at their phones like you see in America ... because Athenians would crash in a heartbeat.

**Not only are the lanes narrow, but you're squeezed in by motorcycles driving between lanes on each side, so my smart car kept warning me of imminent collision. It must have thought I was a complete idiot, but I'm only slightly stoopid.**

Some of the street lines are so faded, you can barely see what lane you're in, which makes negotiating curves terrifying. But not to worry. There are so many cars and motorcycles on each side that they are the lines. You basically follow the herd and hope they don't drive off a cliff.

The street lines, when they're visible, are more like suggestions. You can pass around two lines, no problem. But in ten-plus hours of driving, I haven't seen a single car pulled over by police. Could be a coincidence. Maybe it's the live-and-let-live mentality, which was born in Greece. Maybe they attract more repeat tourists, and the revenue they generate, by not doling out tickets all the time. In any case, the speed limit is also optional.

Watch out for the street lights too. Sometimes they're hidden behind telephone poles or other barriers, not hovering over the middle of the road like American stoplights. They could be easy to miss, but a healthy fear of impending death tends to pump you full of adrenaline and heightened awareness.

And shame on the dudes wearing helmets while their ladies sit on the back of their motorcycles without any protection. And no joke, but one chick was wearing her helmet on her arm, like she was protecting her elbow.

I don't want to end on a negative note, so I'll say this. I finally understand why Greeks are so smart. It's survival of the fittest out here. It's one of the most conquered lands on Earth. The strong survive and it's not your elbows that you need. This marble jungle requires intelligence.

My brain drives at the speed of countryside. It's beautiful. A wee bit queasy for the kids, with all the winding mountain roads, but nothing a little Tummy Soother or a little bungalow in the sand can't fix. You don't need cars on the beach. We love it here.

Long story short: Unless you're an adrenaline junkie, get a cab in the Athens city center, then close your eyes and pray. There are several Greek gods to choose from.

Or you could just hop on a couple velociraptors. They're much safer.

"Riding Dinos"

## Good talk

July 2, 2023

My belly just made a noise that sounded like someone saying "Heyyy." I genuinely thought I had butt-dialed someone, so I put the phone up to my ear and said "Hello?" When my stomach responded with a bunch of gibberish I realized who (or what) I'd been talking to.

"Good talk."

# Thermopylae hot springs

July 11, 2023 | 14 y, 4 mo

**Sure, it smelled like rotten eggs, but the 5-star reviews tell you it's all part of the experience. As soon as I opened the door, a wave of sulfur slapped me.**

Teen 1: "OMG! I am NOT getting in there."

We had just rolled up to some natural baths along the roadside. Several families were enjoying themselves. An old man was standing beneath a waterfall fed by hot springs. We were in the middle of a lush valley, the sacred burial grounds where King Leonidas and his 300 Spartans fought in the Battle of Thermopylae.

Me: "Sulphur is great for your skin. It'll get rid of your zits. Seriously."

Teen 2: "I don't care. It smells awful."

Me: "Alright, whatever. Y'all can stay in the car."

So I jumped out and hopped in. The temperature felt wonderful, up to 104° they say in certain spots. One stretch of the riverbed consisted of smooth rock covered in a thick blanket of algae. When I sat down, it was so slick that I could scoot forward and slide five or more feet at a time. It was fun. I basically looked like a dog scratching its butt on the driveway, but faster and more competitive. Like, I kept trying to beat my previous distance.

There was a nice-looking lady up ahead, stretched out on her back in the middle of the stream. She looked peaceful with her eyes closed, warm water gliding across her face. But as I approached, the current suddenly picked up, so I had to break hard and swerve. It was close. She probably didn't expect to see someone dog-scooting so close to her face, because when I slid by, she opened her eyes and screamed.

"Ahhhhhhhhhooooh my God?!?"

What a sweet siren she was. I expected more, though; a lullaby, some jaggedy rocks maybe.

In retrospect, I don't think you're supposed to make eye contact with anyone when you're doing the dog scoot. It's like solitaire. You play with yourself. If people catch you scootin' about willy-nilly, you'll start doing a lot of things all by your lonesome.

I escaped the witches' eyes, but now everyone else was staring at me too. It was a perplexing look, like they were trying to figure out if what I was doing looked fun or stupid. Sometimes it's a fine line.

It was stupid fun! Then I saw the 4-foot drop-off coming up.

Everyone could see that I was approaching a big cataract. But instead of plunging to my destruction, I lunged for the rope that someone had strung up across the river for this very occasion. From the rope, it was an easy army climb down to the bank.

Me: "Wahoo!!! Who's next? Anybody?"

Apparently, nobody else was preparing for the Summer Games. The hundred-meter scoot has got my ass written all over it. Literally. With all the exfoliation going on up there, you're bound to leave a little butt behind.

**The hormonally challenged little people finally got out of the car. I must have inspired them to live in the moment, or at least pretend for Tik Tok. They knew the dog scoot had meme potential.**

Except my trunks were dark green, so the giant slime stain was camouflaged. It was MUCH more embarrassing on their butts; more like a warning to all the tourists to forego the scoot that I was trying to cajole everyone into.

Maybe I was the siren.

Me: "C'mon, y'all. You gotta try it."

Tourist 1: "Let's not and say we did."

Tourist 2: "Don't look. He's making eye contact!"

When Finn and Fiona finally pointed out their butts to each other, it got awkward. They strategically skedaddled backward so as not to show their asses, but the strategy backfired because it involved looking at people (with their "encouraging" smiles and the creepy old-man wink).

It took a few heavy washes with OxiClean to dissolve the slime, but this one will forever be stained in our brains.

## Abominable snowman
July 18, 2023

Every good vacation should have a running joke that gets bigger and funnier every year. I was the joke in Delphi.

After we dropped our bags off at the Airbnb, we had a delicious seafood dinner overlooking the Gulf of Corinth. Afterward, on the walk back, we bumped into a tourist and his son in the alley next to our place. Melina asked him what his favorite memory was so far on his trip. He looked baffled, like when someone asks me, "What's your favorite band?" He simply extended his hands and exclaimed, "This! I mean … just look around. It's happening."

I understood what he meant. Each moment was a climax, the culmination of all, a continuum of awe. Or maybe he was talking about Melina. She was one of my favorite memories too.

But if he was merely talking about the stairs we were standing on, I would have believed it. We were walking on white marble with thick ribbons of silver and pewter flowing through the alabaster white steps – half-steps, to be precise. And they didn't go straight up, but zigzagged … because in Delphi, nobody's in a hurry. The small town sits high on Mount Parnassus, overlooking beauty in all directions. Every route is the scenic route. It's why Delphics put benches in their alleys. Because homes are covered in trellises full of flowers. Because you should stop and watch the sunset over the Gulf of Corinth.

A few miles away, down in the valley by the water, you can spot two small towns: Itea and Galaxidi. At dusk, their lights flicker like it's Game Seven, bottom of the ninth, bases loaded, 2 outs. Here comes the pitch. Thousands of cameras flash. It's similar to the pattern you see at the bottom of a swimming pool, except instead of the water warping the light, it's the atmosphere that sprinkles fairy dust over the earth and twinkles the night. This happens every evening in Delphi … but only if you stop to enjoy it.

I remember Cousin Georgios asking Melina, "Why do you worry about time? Don't worry about time. What is time?" He was half joking, but also reminding us to stop, look, listen … feel.

Our Airbnb hosts made sure we enjoyed our stay. The dad and daughter rent out their second-story apartment and live below. They immediately felt like family. The old man didn't speak English, so he played charades with us until we understood what he was talking about, usually something about his garden. He always had a smile, like he was juggling a few jokes in his head but knew they'd fall on ignorant ears. And then there was his daughter, Sini. She was beautiful, inside and out, and made an incredible tour guide with local secrets that the almighty Google doesn't even know about.

She also welcomed us with fresh-baked bread – had a whole spread laid out on the kitchen table with olives from their family orchard, several breakfast options, and ripe fruit. They even invited us to sample their liquor cabinet: "It will help you sleep!"

So I did. I couldn't read the labels, so I don't know what I was drinking, but it was strong with a sweet finish. Something you sip slowly. It worked too. Of course, as soon as my head hit the pillow, Melina asked me to get something from the car.

**I thought to myself, "It's 1 a.m. Nobody will see me out there in my undies."**

So I ran out to the car in my underwear, but on the way back, I saw a dark shadow of a person walking toward me. I was standing under a street light, but as I walked forward, the shadow stopped. I would have too if I saw me. I couldn't help but wonder who was more afraid – me of the dark figure or they of the half-naked ginger. I didn't want to find out, so I ran inside.

When I told Melina what happened, Fiona overheard us from her room and hollered her two cents: "They probably thought you were the Abominable Snowman!"

"Ohhhhhh snap, that's cold." It took them a while to get their giggles out at my expense. I'm sure I'll get a nickname out of it. I think they've settled on "Snowginger."

I'll never live it down. As I mentioned in the beginning, it'll start growing tentacles over time.

**"... and then Granddude went streaking through the hills of Mount Parnassus with a herd of hobbits!"**

# 14

# Spoiler: It Was
# Not a Good Idea

## A Bathroom Duel on Corporate Commodes

Aug. 9, 2023

One day, I was in the restroom stall at work when a whistler walked in mid-melody, but stopped short to spare the guy at the urinal.

It bothered me. His unfinished melody was just hanging there and needed to come back home to the tonic, so I did the reasonable thing and whistled off the rest of the riff.

There was a brief pause as the man contemplated. On the one hand, there was bathroom etiquette. On the other, I had challenged him to a duel. My clairvoyance picked up an inaudible "Fuck it" before he proceeded to whistle the next line, continuing the call-and-response from the toilet next door.

Our corporate commodes lived in rooms with four walls, so I could comfortably whistle my freak flag in private. My purple shoes would have been dead giveaways under normal stalls. The high ceilings gave us cathedral-grade reverb, basically turning the tiles into our backing choir. We traded solos loud and proud, sometimes incorporating multiple orifices at once for percussive punctuation.

At some point it got a little too weird, even by my standards, and it occurred to me that I should probably bounce before Dude was done. I don't think either of us wanted to know who the other weirdo was on the other side of the wall.

But there wasn't a clear victor. I needed closure, so I broke out the big guns. I had saved my ace in the hole, a warble that took years to perfect. My tweet rivaled the sweetest of songbirds — less melody and more free-form jazz. I went on for a few measures before whirling to a stop with a dissonant dual tone that I learned from Jim Carrey in The Truman Show — when he was drawing on the mirror, making flying-saucer sounds.

Try it out: just hum and whistle at the same time. If you do it right, the dueling harmonics are super eerie and can clear a room in no time. My dog hated that noise and would scold me if I broke it out.

Urinal guy ran for the hills when my stall started sounding like the hub of an alien spacecraft.

There was no response. I waited for some kind of concession — applause, a groan, anything. All I got was the fluorescent hum. I couldn't tell if the silence was the "sound" of defeat or if my neighbor was just contemplating his next move…

"Plop."

It was done. He was pooped.

There wasn't a mic to drop, so I flushed the toilet.

As I finished washing my hands, relishing in the weirdest victory ever, the most wonderful sounds began floating out of the whistler's stall. They reminded me of the nightingales that lulled me to sleep in Macedonia.

Celestial sounds were dancing across the ceramic-tiles. As I was walking out, the now-distinguished gentleman slipped in a few trills that would have twisted my tongue right off. The door slammed behind me, sealing the verdict.

There was no question. He beat me.

But can you ever truly defeat a whistler?

Whistling while you work isn't just for show. It's an assertion of self in a place built to strip you down to a role. You might be able to out-spreadsheet the whistler, but you can't silence them.

Another existential ritual is the workplace shit. It's one of the few officially sanctioned pauses from performance, a small private place where the day's metrics fall away and you get to be messy, human, honest. In that stall, for two minutes, you rehearse ideas, invent jokes, and plan your escape from corporate life. Add the workplace whistle to your corporate constitution and you've carved out a little pocket of self-sovereignty.

So sure, he beat me on sound. He won the duel. But he didn't win at what counts, which is the capacity to be undeterred, to keep making noise. That's a victory we share with every whistler alike, with all the good men who rage against the dying of the light. A victory you can't tick off on a performance review.

When we got back to our desks, an impromptu meeting request had arrived in our inboxes  – a drop-everything, all-hands-on-deck kinda thing.

So we all piled into the conference room and hopped on the call. Our CMO got right to business announcing $300 million dollars in layoffs – just in time for Christmas. Nothing says holiday spirit like Santa outsourcing the elves to Bangladesh.

None of us were about to go back to work, so we decided to grab lunch. As we got into the van, the colleague next to me began to hum a familiar tune, and I had no choice but to finish him off. We looked up at each other like long-lost brothers, separated by tractor beams at birth.

I wanted to give the guy a hug, but it was a delicate situation. We both knew that if one of us started laughing or confronted the other weirdo, then we'd have to tell the story to everyone. So we shut the hell up. It was our little secret.

His secret, rather. I've no shits to give.

## Shot for my head

Sept. 2, 2023

Earlier this evening, I got shot in the butt and passed out. The lady told me to pull my pants down, which I wasn't expecting. It didn't make sense. The last thing I remember was asking, "What's happening?" After that it was lights out. Apparently, my muscles spasmed, which triggered a fight-or-flight response. Basically, my butt told my brain to play possum.

When I woke up, I couldn't figure out why I was looking up into some dude's nose. It was a big schnoz – even bigger because it was three inches from my face.

My first thought was about how awkward it would get if I didn't say something to lighten the mood, but I couldn't think of anything. It's like thousands of words were lost somewhere in my head. I knew they were there, but I couldn't form a single sentence.

Why was this strange man gazing into my eyes? Where was I? I felt like he owed it to me to break the silence because it's rude to stare. Like, you got a problem with me, Mr. Lab Coat? Those nostrils look like they could use some maintenance. Then it all came flooding back: who I was, why I was there, who it was who clearly needed a nose-hair trim.

Doctor Addison explained everything while I followed his finger with my eyes. After I aced the current-affairs quiz, he asked how I was feeling.

"Well, I've got a big lump on my head, but at least the shot got rid of the pain in my neck."

Thankfully, it was a small room and the wall broke most of the fall. I didn't hit too hard, just got a little banged up.

**The nurse was a noob. She should have had me lie on the examining-room table or at least bend over it, but she probably got distracted when I dropped trou. My buns have that effect on people.**

My ass was also confused. Why was it getting the shot when my neck was the fucked–up body part? No wonder my butt froze up and panicked. The nurse explained that this steroid shot was a temporary measure until they could schedule a longer-lasting epidural injection in my spinal cord. Like a sawed-off shotgun, the butt/buck-shot sprays wide and destroys inflamation throughout the body, whereas the epidural is a sniper that kills the pain precisely where it stands.

"I don't suppose you have another shot for my head, do you?"

I gave the Doctor a wink. I always wanted to do that. A good doctor always has a twinkle in their eye – always a snappy one-liner to make you feel better as they walk out the door.

"Nice try, buddy."

## Flirtatious farting doesn't work
Oct. 5, 2023

**I dropped the biggest bomb at Planet Fitness and OMG ... the poor girl. She walked right into it.**

Me: "I thought you could reset the infrared sauna from the lobby. I've seen y'all do it before. I wouldn't have told you that it wasn't working if I knew you were going in there. I am soooooo sorry for that."

Cutie at the counter: "Oh no! Why?"

Me: "Oh come on. You know. I just ... farted right before you went in and it was really bad."

Cutie: "Hahaha!"

Me: "It might have been the reason your machine broke."

Cutie: "Hahaha!"

Me: "I might have killed a fly. It was just lying there."

Cutie: "Hahaha."

Me: "Hopefully it was just in shock."

Cutie: "Get out of here!"

Me: "You can't tell me you didn't smell that."

Cutie: "I'll smell ya later. Now go!"

Me: "Okay, see ya! Have a good one. Hey, I'm blowing you a kiss right now."

Cutie: "What?"

Me: "Just wait a sec. It's coming."

Cutie: "OMG! Gross!"

She ran out of the room. Aaaaand this is why my wife doesn't worry about me flirting.

# A good omen

I shared this story with a friend today and felt like y'all should read it because one, it's hilarious and two, I really need to sit down after smoking that Cuban.

This message is brought to you by Montecristo Robustos and dedicated to Melina's dad, the late, great Vasili, or Papou to Finn and Fiona. He passed them down to me and always enjoyed a good laugh between tokes.

In March 2009, I started working for United Methodist Communications as a digital marketer. A few days into my new job, I had to deliver a memo to someone whom I hadn't met. I won't drop her name, but she was a kind, gregarious woman, close to retiring, and always had the sweetest smile.

As I walked up to her cubicle, I could see her searching for content in a stock photography site. Just as the words "Excuse me" left my mouth, she clicked the next button and swiveled around. As she turned to face me, the page loaded and up popped a black-and-white family portrait.

Of course there's a catch. Everyone was buck naked! The picture was a parody of vintage photographs from the 1800s when camera exposures took so long to capture the light, that nobody wanted to fake a smile for that long. So the whole family is completely serious, just standing there with saggy … earlobes amongst other things.

Normally I can put on a pretty good poker face, but my superpowers were no match for this. I kept my composure, but it didn't take long for her to notice that my eyes were darting back and forth between her and the naked people. My state of distraction eventually becomes so obvious that the sweet church lady swivels back around.

"What are you looking AAAAHHHH!?!"

The lady about broke her hand as she slammed it down, clicking frantically until the cursor found its way to the X button. Then the poor little church mouse swore up and down she had never looked at anything like that in her entire life. I told her to stop being ridiculous, that she didn't need to apologize or be ashamed about anything.

It was a good omen: a sign from God that my weirdness would be welcome.

## If a prayer falls in the woods
Nov. 25, 2023

Even though I'm agnostic, I still believe prayer works. I still wishfully hope for magic in the sky, but I can't deny science, or scientific "testimonies" if you will.

Studies on prayer have been heavily researched. The more controlled, higher-sampled ones have been synthesized to form a meta-analysis, which is the gold standard of research. And of course, all papers that are included essentially find a statistically significant benefit if you are praying for yourself or know that a group is praying for you. This makes complete sense. Anyone in that situation would be more hopeful or relaxed and not want to give up, unless knowing they're being prayed for makes them bitter because they aren't a believer. I feel bad for them.

But if you don't know anyone is praying for you, when there are indeed people praying for you, there are no statistically significant benefits. I'm not making a claim about God and neither are the studies. I'm just saying maybe God doesn't heal people just because we ask. Maybe we have no earthly idea how God acts and shouldn't try to make claims about God's nature.

Maybe God wanted prayer to be communal and done together all along. Maybe God designed prayer to be completely scientific and he's largely hands-off. Maybe everything's happening according to free will, momentum, and laws of nature.

Maybe God designed prayer to only affect our psychoneuroimmunological pathways when it's observed by other people. Photons act differently when they're observed, so why not humans at prayer? Maybe distant prayer only benefits the person who's praying from afar. There has to be a meditative benefit even if they're praying for someone else. It certainly makes them feel good. At least, this is what all the studies suggest. Maybe God wanted us to stay and pray together, stay connected to each other.

Regardless of what anyone believes, these results suggest that we should be directly involved with the people and missions we love and believe in. Your voice, your touch, your financial contributions can be healing. You can pray from afar and never talk to the person you're praying for, but that could also be an excuse for being a lazy friend. I'm just saying that in addition to praying for disaster-torn people, why not also send blankets, food and water?

I'm thankful if you're thinking of me. But if I don't hear your prayer falling in the woods, I hope you meant it and it does something good for you. Thank you for being your best self. I pray your ripple effect will someday make its way back.

I'm pretty sure trees are sad when they feel one of their own go down. Similarly, I don't think prayers from afar are offered in vain. Everything is felt, big or little, physical or mental. All ONE … eventually.

## Me and my ego
Jan. 4, 2024

I hate to admit that I snore, but the other night it woke my ass up. We were at one of the big family Christmas parties. Everyone was having a ball, myself included, except I had reached my people quota for the day. So I retreated into a guest bedroom to meditate.

Falling asleep would be a lame party foul, but getting under the covers and snuggling with a soft body pillow seemed like a good idea. Clearly, my internal idiot alerts were on vacation too because I went down like the light switch that I had just flipped.

Next thing I knew, semi-nude fairies from FernGully were floating above me. The dream was heavenly until this loud snort barged in and crashed the party. So I jumped up, hit the nog like a good Christmas elf, and joined in on the family festivities.

Now, I freely admit that I snore because we've all reclassified it as a superpower. We call it the Anti-Ass Snoring System. And by "we," with apologies to the late Harry Nilsson, I mean ...

> Me and my Ego
> Straighter than narrow
> Wherever we go
> Everyone knows
> It's me and my Ego

Melina aptly calls it ASS, for short.

Now if I can just get back to the rainforest. Lucid dreams about fairies don't count as cheating, do they? I think as long as you keep it 2-D, we can call it a loophole.

Speaking of naughty Christmas wishes ...

"Christmas Tree"

## Olympic Shopping Trolley
Jan. 5, 2024

**If you're looking for something with plenty of speed and good handling, try the shopping carts at Target.**

They must oil the wheels, 'cause those suckers fly. They're hot rods compared to everything else on the market. I'm tired of the sticky wheels at Walmart. One time I veered off course and crashed into some beans. Those displays come out of nowhere, like ninjas, jumping out to surprise you with their BOGO bean prices.

Anyway, if you've never hopped a cart, you're not living your best life. Listen, you have my permission to be a kid again. Jump up and coast down an aisle or two. Steering is easy. Just put your foot down on one wheel at a time. Break the right wheel to turn right, left wheel to turn left.

People will point and stare, admiring your mastery. "Look, Johnny. That man-child has complete control over his vehicle! Did you see the way he negotiated around the beans?"

We've already submitted the sport to the Summer Olympics Committee under the category "Shopping Trolley." They told us teams of two are required, so if you want to be the person inside, I'll push. And we'll need to get under 20 seconds in the 100-meter dash. The world record is 14.33, so every millisecond counts. You'll need to shave your head to be fully aerodynamic. PM me if you're interested.

## 919 Island Cuisine
Jan. 12, 2024

After work I picked up some grub at 919 Island Cuisine, then hurried home to feed the 14-year-olds who were surely dying of hunger. As I drove through back country roads, just minutes away, a deer bolted out of the woods and took the leap. But instead of slowing down, I made the correct choice and grabbed the beef pies. It would have been gruesome if they flew out of the bag. I rescued those pies and I'd do it again, no regrets. You try going home to hungry lions empty-handed. Good luck!

Thankfully, I was able to hit the brakes just in time. It was a close call, but the pies were safe … at least until I got home and tossed them into the den. Now that was a bloody massacre. But at least it was quick. Those poor beef pies never saw it coming.

The lion's den.

## Sunday soccer

Oct. 15, 2024

Fiona's goalie. I'm hanging out on the sideline near midfield where parents from both teams are in close proximity. Butts collide on the field and it appears like one of our girls was a bit aggressive.

Soccer Mom: "Way to go!"

Soccer Dad: [Whispering] "The other parents can hear you."

Soccer Mom: "Well, it's a contact sport. This is how you play."

Soccer Dad: "It's Sunday baby. It's a holy day."

Me: "She's like, 'take her out!' lol."

Soccer Dad: "I know, right?"

Me: "In light of it being a holy day, maybe it wasn't a hip-check. Maybe she was merely turning the other cheek ... really quickly. And the other team needs to give our girls enough space to do that or else we're gonna turn-the-other-cheek 'em into the ground."

Soccer Mom: "Amen!"

Other-team parent: "We can hear you."

Soccer Mom: "Preach it!"

## The wonderful world of Willow
Oct. 19, 2024

"Stop the car!" cried Willow! "Pull over here," my sister continued frantically.

Mom quickly pulled off and parked in front of an orthodontist office sitting inside a retail strip mall.

"What's going on?" Mom inquired.

There was no time to explain. Willow exploded out of the car, sprinted across the parking lot, then charged a minivan that was about to take off, yelling "STOOOOOP!"

The soccer mom was either won over by Willow's calming countenance or afraid for her life. Either way, she didn't run her over as Willow got on all fours.

**"There's a kitty next to your tire!"**

The lady looked relieved that she hadn't run anything over and that Willow was merely a crazy cat lady and not a total whacko.

The tiny tortoise shell was quivering, couldn't have been more than a pound – clearly malnourished by the looks of her ribs sticking out. When Willow reached under the vehicle, the little kitty took off, then hightailed it through a sea of cars, disappearing into an overgrown wooded area at the far end of the strip.

Hot in pursuit, Willow ran into the bramble, crawled through a thicket of thorns, traversed down a ravine full of poison ivy, fell into a legit quagmire, sunk down to her knees, almost lost a flip-flop in the muck, was scratched and bloodied and muddied, but by golly, Willow crawled out of that bush with a cat!

Willow was well aware that feral cats won't let you kittynap them without first putting up a fight. This wasn't her first rodeo. She was getting sliced open, bitten, hissed at – almost dropped the thing until she instinctively placed the little beasty over her bosom. As soon as she heard a heartbeat, the little furball melted into Momma and calmed down. She was home.

Meanwhile, Mom and Grandma were thoroughly confused, waiting in their car. When Willow walked up toting the tortoise shell, they didn't question the mud or the blood or the leaves in her hair. It made perfect sense. Just another day in the life of the Wonderful World of Willow. And now, Tiki. Tiki Cummerbund Quagmire Jones, that is.

## Speaking of quagmires ...
Oct. 20, 2024

… I lost a very important purple shoe at the bottom of one.

Melina's family from Raleigh was visiting us in Nashville, so I was on my best behavior, trying not to do anything stupid. Around lunchtime, I was coming back from Calypso Cafe, heading towards Centennial Park where everyone was waiting by the Parthenon for a nice family picnic. As I power walked across the park, I made a split decision to shave a few minutes off the delivery. I could have walked around the lake like a normal person, but this particular summer, the universe had programmed a little Easter Egg into my "game," a shortcut that would surely impress my soon-to-be in-laws.

A few months back, city renovators had drained the lake for a big beautification project. Afterwards, the summer sun had baked the basin floor dry.

"Aces!"

So I jumped down off the cement ledge surrounding the basin and cruised across the "lake." I wasn't walking on water, but by God, I was delivering that Jerk Chicken with God speed.

The normies walking the perimeter were all telling their children not to get any "bright" ideas. Then I fell into a quagmire and felt everyone's collective condemnation.

"See Johny. That's why you don't cut corners. Fucking quagmires will getcha every time."

Apparently, the basin floor wasn't completely dry. Below the thin layer of baked mud was actual mud, and lots of it.

"A little help?!?" I suggested to a family walking by.

They ignored my plea – probably afraid that I'd pull them in. I couldn't use my hands to get out because they were carrying four giant bags of food that I was not about to set in the mud. The muck was similar to quicksand insomuch that when I lifted one foot, the other foot sank further down.

Any movement accelerated the sinking. "I'm going to die in a quagmire," I said to myself.

Mel's family was likely within earshot, so shouting for help was not an option. It was at that point that I had a moment of clarity. Instead of struggling, I stood still. A few seconds later, the sinking stopped. My ego was suffocating, but at least my lungs would be pumping oxygen for the foreseeable future and not fish poop.

It didn't take long before a gentleman ran out to lend a hand. The guy was a genuine human being, undeterred by the danger of drowning in slow motion.

He didn't look native to Nashville, towering over me, wearing a warm smile and a brightly colored tunic pulled over his shoulder. My angel had huge hands that engulfed mine. Pulling me out seemed effortless as he leaned his center of gravity back over solid ground, giving me just enough leverage to lift my feet out without the two of us breaking through the crust.

After much gratitude and a big bear hug, I said goodbye and then sludged around the "lake" to feed the fam. And by sludged, I mean strutted my stuff with scum up to my knees and four pristine white bags in my hands. My gait was off kilter due to one of my shoes slipping off in the muck. Once again, I played it off like victory swagger. Besides, it was a good opportunity to practice my pimp walk.

The drowning of my purple shoe was a tragic loss. He was a good shoe, faithful to the end. I could have tossed his twin so as not to waddle like a penguin, but I wasn't ready to part ways so soon after the fall of his fraternal brother. People would swear they looked identical, but one was left-footed while the other was wrong. We all knew Lefty would outlast his brother. Poor Wrongfoot. He was doomed before his first step.

Which is why it was better for my soon-to-be in-laws to see the real me. The world's already overflowing with fake – with quagmires that look solid on the surface but are full of muck underneath.

Better to get it all out early, set the bar low so that anything short of idiocracy would feel like a warm welcome. I'd rather be an occasional surprise than a perpetual fuck-up.

# 15

# Don't Die with the **Music in You**

## Peaceful parenting

Nov. 4, 2024

I know, this is too long for the average attention span. But if you can't stop your child's temper tantrums, stick with me. If you are a new parent, this is important. You can also forward this piece using the QR code at the end if you know someone who should read this.

I'd like to share my shortcomings and successes in an attempt to provide an alternative to corporal punishment. I won't make a moral case against spanking here. Instead, my hope is to show that peaceful parenting is more efficient.

If you think spanking is okay, I hope you'll consider the system below as a supplement. It can't hurt (literally), and I'm proud to say it has worked well for us. We're not perfect, and I regret the short period we did spank, but there are lessons for those who don't have to make the same mistakes.

## Our experience

I've done a ton of research on the topic and have lived through fifteen years with fraternal twins. I've had the unique opportunity to A/B test spanking and other systems on two completely different personalities. I've learned that every method is flawed unless custom modifications are made for individual personalities. So my first piece of advice is to take it all with a grain of salt.

## Background

When we began spanking, our twins were about 3 years old. Immediately, I noticed a correlation to my twins hitting each other. Naturally they modeled my example and thought it was the way to deal with each others' bad behavior.

After I learned what spanking does to the developing brain, I stopped immediately and began researching a whole new system. It took some reverse engineering, but eventually my kids stopped hitting each other, became better friends, and still like each other to this day. (Update: As of this edit, they're 16 and still say goodnight to each other.)

I'd like to note that I recognize parents who try to ethically spank. I know a few who do this and have raised wonderful children. But one, even ethical spanking can easily get out of control and two, it's not effective. Because an ethical spank/mild pat on the butt doesn't deliver the message and would probably be preferred over severe consequences – or as I like to put it, "an offer that can't be refused."

But enough background. Here's how it works.

## The system

After consulting a few books and several podcasts, I created a system that gradually became harder as behavior improved. Basically, you put a whiteboard up on the fridge, then write a list of a few bad behaviors that you'd like your kids to work on. Think of the things that annoy you the most and work on them first. If they exhibit any of those behaviors, put an X on the board.

One X is just a warning. We all have bad days and deserve a little grace up front. Two Xs need to be addressed. Consequences will need to be different for each child, but consider taking something special away like dessert, toys, or privileges (e.g. permission to go on a playdate, play video games or watch TV). Severe consequences are crucial because timeouts are usually a waste of time. Once, when I was a child, I actually asked to be spanked, in lieu of a timeout, so that I could get it over with and go play.

Three Xs in one day should result in an "offer they can't refuse." The base-level consequence began with early bedtime, as in right after dinner. Additional Xs could lead to a full week of early bedtime, taking toys away (up to and including everything in their room), no playtime with friends, no access to devices, etc. These consequences are actually worse than a few pops on the bottom.

### Natural consequences

Use a little psychology to transfer their anger away from you toward their own culpability. Instead of making early bedtime sound like a punishment (a kind of jail sentence), focus on natural consequences. Tell your kids that doctors are like bosses for parents; parents have to listen to them or else they're not doing their jobs. Explain that when kids misbehave, it's often because they're tired and grumpy, so Doc said you just need to take a nap.

"If you don't go to bed early, our family will pay high costs from sickness and stress, which will drastically reduce the money we've saved for toys. We have to follow doctor's orders, because our health keeps us alive. We're bummed out too, but this is the reason for early bedtime. You can choose to stay awake or turn the lights back on, but those actions will result in the removal of all your toys from your room. The doctor said it's crucial to get your rest, so that tomorrow your brain can deal with stress."

Just saying, "Go to your room!" teaches them nothing and will add to their ever-increasing contempt toward your authority and worldview. "Because I said so" is not an explanation. It's a phrase that should only be uttered if you're running an army base. Take the time up front to explain how the world works and your kids will learn that there are logical solutions to problems. They'll also value your opinion and come to you for advice later in life.

We've used the doctor hack hundreds of times in many other situations (vegetables, exercise, and more). It works without fail because it not only validates what you're saying via the higher power, but also shifts their resentment to the doctor and away from you. Eventually, they learn whatever it is they don't feel like doing isn't something to get angry over. Having to do things you don't want to do, or when you don't want to do them, is just part of life. When you're unmotivated or uncooperative, the healthy response is to: 1. Take advice from doctors; and 2. Take a nap.

## Custom modifications

Like I said earlier, every system has flaws and must be tailored to the individual. I noticed that early bedtime began to be ineffective for Finn. Maybe he learned the lesson that tired = grumpy = bedtime. Maybe he just didn't mind the extra rest. I already knew timeouts never fazed him. He'd just sing to himself or ponder the secret mysteries of the universe, the latter being something he did most of the time anyway. Fiona, by contrast, loathed timeouts.

In the end, I learned to take away what each of them loved the most. For Finn, it was books and video games. For Fiona, it was relationships, people, and family time. For our dog, Piper, it was the poo she rolled in. She hated when I cleaned that shit off.

## The rule of three

It's crucial that you only work on two or three bad behaviors at once. This exact number could be more or less, depending on maturity level, but the idea is if you focus on more than three behaviors the system will fail, especially when one behavior is particularly challenging.

One time, I took all three behaviors off the list and made "not listening" the sole focus because it drove me crazy and it was too easy to get three X's by disobeying that one rule. In general, if you pile on too many bad behaviors, your kids will realize the system is unbeatable.

For this system to work, you have to be tough but fair. Adjust the numbers of prohibited behaviors and the number of Xs allowed as necessary, so that your kids don't become apathetic. They'll act out just to say, "Screw you and your unbeatable system." For other bad behaviors that weren't on our list (and there were many at first), I'd either ignore them if they were minor or punish with timeouts. So timeouts can play a small part in the system, but as the primary go-to, they were mostly ineffective.

Be patient. It takes about three to six weeks to conquer one bad behavior, at which time you erase and replace. One down. Next problem.

### Nervous ticks

Chewing fingernails is one of those habits that you completely ignore. One syndicated columnist, named John Rosemond, instructs parents to not put that one on the list. It's actually a coping mechanism that helps children deal with stress. Take it away and you could actually cause more petty fights and frustration. Rosemond recommends letting your child have that one. Many children stop this or other nervous tics when they become more comfortable with life. Finn quit biting his nails around 8 years old after I made him a $50 bet that he couldn't stop for a month straight. He won.

### Lying

It's one behavior that doesn't work with the X system. Rosemond suggests that you almost completely ignore it. "Almost" because you should at least address the issue. It seems counterintuitive, but it worked for us. The most you have to say is "Don't lie" or "I don't want to hear it" and walk away. Never fight it. Shut it down. Don't try to catch them in a lie or attempt to reason. Don't give them the slightest clue it's upsetting. Even if you prove them wrong, there may still be an agonizing, time-consuming back-and-forth fight. When those kinds of fights become routine, they learn they have power over you, to break you down and inflict stress. What's worse, they learn that sometimes lying works. If it helps them get off the hook, they'll fight for it every time, even if the odds are slim.

Go with your gut. Ninety-five percent of the time, if you have a solid reason to believe they're lying, you are right. Five-year-old psychology is pretty easy to see through. And if you fight with them, they learn to punish you when they feel like it. Don't punish them for lying unless it's really bad. You be the judge. But in real life, liars lose relationships and people stop taking them seriously. So mirror this natural phenomenon.

We had a short phase, but I ignored my son's lies for about a month when he was 5 and that phase has never resurfaced. I didn't believe he made up the jokes. I knew the jokes he made up and I knew the ones he plagiarized. The jokes he made up were actually funny (for a 5 year old) and the ones he stole, I had heard. I simply said, "Those jokes are funny, but you can't tell me that you made it up. Stop copying." He fussed. I said, "We're not having this conversation," and walked away. He lied in a few other areas and if I had a good hunch, I discounted everything he said. He was furious.

And he may have been telling the truth a few times, in terms of which stories and jokes he had made up himself. In light of that possibility, I explained that he would be getting one and only blanket "sorry" for those times, but otherwise, "Don't give me that crap. I've got better things to do." He learned quickly how much it sucks when your voice isn't heard and when your stories don't matter. It was a problem, but since then, I can count on one hand the times he's lied. Fiona has always told the truth, so I never had to worry about it.

## Hitting

Hitting (outside of defense) doesn't have to be on the list. It will always result in three X's and a severe consequence. Do not tolerate violence. I've been known to take every toy away for a week or a phone away for three months.

That said, if you watch my kids wrestle or play at karate, you might think they have no mercy. But look closely and you'll see quite a bit of restraint. First of all, they've been practicing how to kick each other in the head since the womb. Second, as a family we play-fight all the time, so they understand the rules. "Stop!" means stop and hitting out of anger is not permitted. The boundaries can be tough to manage, but like any other sport it requires practice. You learn to respect your opponent, even if it's for selfish reasons. It's fun to have fun and you don't want things to get out of hand or game over. Speaking of which …

"Gladiator funboards"

## Keep calm

Aside from insignificant coping mechanisms, small annoyances, and lying, stick to the system. And never let them know you're upset, even when they're hitting. This rule applies across the board. Never yell or get mad when you administer consequences. You might think it's effective, but it actually gives them power and in the long run, the upper hand. In life, there are consequences to bad behavior and they must feel the full brunt of their actions.

If you add yelling to the mix, then some children may act out just to get a rise out of you. For some children, yelling adds resentment to the equation, so they won't even be upset at the consequence – they'll be mad at you for embarrassing them in front of people. If you say what will happen calmly or take them aside and explain what will happen later, they only have themselves to blame. Keep the pain centered on them. Take the monkey off your back.

I even created safeguards around this prohibition. If I yelled at them, all they had to do was point it out and not only would the consequence be nullified, I would owe them a dollar. I also clearly defined yelling verse raising my voice and delivering a stern talk. Giving them the power to enforce the rules of a contract will serve you in the long run because they will understand the system is about justice, not arbitrary punishments.

That said, I don't always live up to this rule. I still find myself shouting, because I'm flawed. At the risk of Finn and Fiona hating my existence, I had to create a system to counter my nature. As a result, instead of them feeling powerless or afraid when I yell, they remind me that I need to chill out, that I owe them, and that they don't get an X per the agreement. Instead of yelling, I simply shrug it off and give them an X.

## Stick to the rules

If one out of 100 times you let them off the hook, they'll beg 100% of the time for you to go easy. One out of 100 is still pretty good odds for a child. Administering the consequence 100% of the time results in 0% begging. It takes a little while, but they soon realize begging is futile. Also, keep in mind that begging and arguing are two different things. Arguing is good as long as they're using reason, logic, and evidence. Because we talk about our issues calmly, arguing is something we do regularly. And because we make win–win deals, arguing has become a part of our family culture.

Many times, my children have used my own logic from past arguments to mitigate consequences. I don't ever let them off the hook, but if the logic is sound, I will change my mind. Still, sometimes they just have to stop crying and explain what happened before logic can happen. If you've demonstrated that anger in tough situations is not needed, they'll learn not to cry and shout during tough situations.

I mentioned making deals. Start making win–win deals in almost all interactions. Let them argue and make deals with you. A deal will solve almost 99% of the problems you have with your kids. If they want something out of the ordinary, I make them earn it. If I want something, I promise to play with them for a specific time period. Negotiation is an art that will help them immensely later in life.

If you never falter with the rules, consistency becomes second nature. You begin to see quick results. You create a machine that knocks out bad behaviors with incredible efficiency. They get used to the system and some bad behaviors are eliminated within days. They understand the consequences, and realize that defiance is not worth it.

## Timing

Keep in mind that you'll often be in a location that won't allow for a severe consequence. Again, keep cool, make a mental note and enforce it when you get home. You don't have to enforce anything at the time of the infraction. You don't even have to tell them what will happen if doing so will cause a scene (e.g. ruin dinner at a nice restaurant). Plus, in your anger you may make empty threats you're not prepared to enforce. Just think about it. Store it away. Strategically withhold the consequence until the time is right. Later on, you calmly say, "OK, it's time to go to bed early because XYZ." If you tell them the news before dinner, they may not eat their vegetables. It's all in the timing.

## Evolution and sunset

Finally, it's important for the system to gradually become harder as behavior improves. After a while, three Xs per day becomes easy and the consequences dry up. So we all agreed to change the rule to two Xs per day, then eventually one X per day.

When they were nine years old, I abandoned the X system altogether. One day the kids woke up to see that I erased everything on the whiteboard and replaced it with a big heart. I later explained that we didn't need it anymore. If a bad behavior resurfaced, I would decide at the time what the consequence would be or cut a deal.

## Make a deal

Deals get really creative and are custom-made for the situation. Over time, my kids started to lay out specific requirements for games, playtime, etc. It was amazing to watch and often I wanted to jump in. Don't do it, though. Let them negotiate as much as possible without interfering. In other words, let them set the structure and create rules themselves. This is how you pass the baton.

Recently, Finn came to me one morning with a problem and instead of getting out of bed, I simply said "Make a deal," rolled over, and went back to sleep. Later, I found out that Finn made a deal to play with Fiona for an hour, if she stayed out of the computer room, so he could record his video game screencast in peace and without a bunch of noise in the background. She agreed. As time goes by, the rules or terms are better articulated. As long as we clearly communicate what we want and come to an agreement, then we get what we want.

## Positive versus negative reinforcement

The X system is based on consequences or negative reinforcement, but making win–win deals adds the crucial element of positive reinforcement. Negative reinforcement is more efficient because a child will often forego small rewards so they can continue living comfortably in bad habits. Your system for driving behavioral change cannot be solely based on a reward system. Positive reinforcement must supplement a much more robust system that mirrors real life – which, again, focuses on consequences. You don't always get rewarded for being a good citizen or doing your job, but bad behavior is almost always noticed and there are usually tangible negative consequences.

That said, of course you should create rewards for good behavior. I also reward randomly, to show an occasion, birthday, or holiday aren't requirements for showing love. Of course, reward them when they do outstanding work. This seems obvious, but more important is to stop rewarding mediocrity. Stop saying "That's nice" or "Good job" every time they do something cute. Don't squash dreams, but be honest.

Eventually, they'll see through the "Good-job!" BS. Around that time, they'll also start to ignore you. Tersely replying that school was "good" signals they don't have to be honest – an example you may have set by modeling insincerity. Take off the mask, roll the façade aside and give them honesty. Sometimes it's hard, but they'll come to you for the hard stuff if you're real with them.

Finn and Fiona worked through most of the bad behaviors we targeted. As a result, I stopped giving X's. That lasted for about two years, but we had to start it up again during a bad phase or two. Listening is a constant work in progress. My point here is that you should feel free to stop or start the system as needed. Backsliding happens. New bad habits happen. Your goal is to raise kids who are peaceful, obedient, and trusting of their elders, while retaining skeptical minds. The latter is possible because they're not punished for arguing.

## Unintended consequences of spanking

Some research indicates that spanking may actually lower IQ by two or three points. I posit that children who are regularly hit out of anger look at most adults with fear and contempt. They may not trust teachers because they equate the school's force with the same force of their parents' hands. Constant fear leads to blind obedience, apathy, self-harm and, in many cases, to abuse of others out of identification with the abuser(s). Thus, force begins the gradual decay of our families and school standards.

Many longitudinal (multi-year) studies on spanking that follow children for significant portions of their lives have documented correlations with teen pregnancy, drug use, domestic violence, criminal activity, Type 2 diabetes, cancer, depression, eating disorders and more. Spanking may "work" for docile children. Really, they just live in fear and begin their lives with a chip on their shoulders – a distrust of adults, or those in power. For others it flips a switch in their brains and causes them to rebel, fight, and perpetuate a culture of violence. What do you want your legacy to be?

## Freedom

Give your children choices. Give them peaceful parenting. Hopefully, this will help restore broken relationships and lead to a much happier life. I thought I was losing my children during the short time when we spanked. Their anger and violent behavior got pretty bad for awhile, but thankfully, I discovered this system while researching peaceful parenting.

What do you want the world to be like? One of the roots to this answer starts with peaceful parenting. Please consider sharing this piece. Share the love!

"Share Peaceful Parenting"

## Headlines of hope

Nov. 20, 2024

Corporate media knows the behavioral science – that fear weighs (and pays) twice as much as anything resembling hope. So, of course they're going to sell terror 24-7. But there's another side to the story. For several years, I've collected all the major tech, medical, and energy breakthroughs – real antidotes to despair. In dark times, I hope it shines a light. Help me spread the love.

"Share Headlines of Hope"

## M.C. Escher

Nov. 29, 2024

You know the M.C. Escher piece with the two hands drawing each other? Well I was scratching my dog Piper today and it got sorta weird like that.

There I was, lying on the floor, scratching her belly, when somehow as she started kicking her legs, she started scratching my head at the same time. She had the angle just right. It was really pleasant. It always feels better when someone else does it right? Plus, if you scratch yourself for too long, people may think you're deranged. This happened to me once.

When I was nine, I broke my dad's glasses being careless and he threatened to beat me with a two-by-four. Said I wouldn't be able to sit down for two weeks. He never hit me, ever actually, but just to be sure, I ran away for a day and hid in the woods behind Smith Park. Except I forgot to bring TP, so I came home with poison ivy between my nether cheeks. In retrospect, I would have preferred the two- by-four. I got a lot of strange stares that month and found that honesty was the easiest answer.

"It's poison ivy okay. Want me to show you? I'll do it. No? Then mind your own business." Their stares turned to either pity or laughter, but both were better than being gawked at like a side-show freak.

My dad and his dog Honey Bear

Another time, my dad brought lice home, so my sister Willow thought it would be funny to tell my friends that they couldn't play with me that day because, "Our family has bugs. Sorry. We're gonna get sprayed tonight."

So you see, I have a long and storied history of big itches. Today, my cross-species scratch-a-thon completed a perfect trifecta of epic itches.

There we were, me and my dog on the floor. I was turning my head around so she could get different spots.

"Mmmm, that's good. Right there. Let's hold that. Hold. Hooooooold. Aaaaaaaaand holding still."

It's good to give your dog feedback. Communication is key.

Then it occurred to me that someone could walk in on us and it might look funny. What would I say? I wouldn't have to explain myself to Escher. He would know exactly what we were doing. We were making art.

**The paw that scratches the man who scratches the dog who fetches a beer, represents the eternal bond between man and man's best friend.**

167

That's right. I taught my dog to fetch six packs from the fridge. Everyone had a Covid project and that was mine. I've got the video below to prove it.

It took an incredible amount of dedication and training to accomplish this feat. Afterwards, for some reason, I didn't get much of anything done around the house. To be honest, I don't really recall a whole lot from that period in my life. My wife assures me though, that I was a big pile of monkey dump.

"Man's best friend"

## R.I.P. Piper
Jan. 9, 2025

We had to put Piper down today. 12 years of great health, then one twist of fate, and it had to be done.

She had a wonderful life. We never had to put her on a leash because she always stayed close. Although she never ran away, she always ran off. She'd go on a big adventure every night when we let her out for "Last call!"

Occasionally a neighbor would catch her on their deer cam and post pictures on Nextdoor, concerned for the "LOST DOG!" She was a creature of the night. Nobody could catch her because she only let people from our inner circle get close. I affectionately called her Scooby because she was scared of everyone, especially the boogieman.

So yeah, Piper would run wild in the woods. She was a free dog, which is why she chose to come back. She'd always return about an hour later after she had sniffed all there was to sniff.

She didn't like certain smells to be forced upon her though. She'd run out of the room and bark at me if I farted in her general direction. It's not that she was surprised by the outburst. My dog just thought I was gross. Sometimes she'd protest by going outside and rolling in shit, then prance around gleefully, basically implying that "it" smelled better than me. It was a slap in my face, but I deserved it. She always spoke her mind and I respected her for that.

She liked hearing her voice. That hound dog was the best alarm money could buy. When contractors came to our house, the first order of business was for her to inspect their vehicle for the boogie man. They'd have to open the door so Piper could peek in and give it a quick sniff test. If their van checked out, she'd stop sounding the alarm. It became so routine that a couple guys used to go through the ritual without me having to ask. If we forgot, she'd bark endlessly. Then one of us would drag her inside where she'd continue alerting us of the imminent danger looming in the windowless white van.

The only time she ever bit someone also happened to be the only time she had to rescue said someone from recklessly running off the diving board. Piper was a legit lifeguard and did NOT like rule breakers. The "no running" sign was clearly painted on the gate ... Alex. Surprisingly, the little dude's parents told us not to worry about it. Country folk are cool like that. They understood she was just trying to protect the boy.

You could teach Piper to do just about anything if you had enough peanut butter. At the peak of our training, she pulled the fridge door open using a rag tied to the handle, snatched a six-pack of beer, delivered the beverages to our feet, then promptly ran back to shut the fridge door like a boss.

#MansBestFriend

She was also an expert at catching Scooby snacks. She would never disgrace herself by letting a hot dog hit her in the face. Even when her eyes clouded over and things got fuzzy, her big schnozz would lead her mouth to glory. She was like Willie Mays out there, catching fly wieners.

She knew she was great, and borderline stubborn as a result. She had an air of confidence and carried herself like a queen ... who routinely needed to be reminded of her actual lot in life. Once, Finn and Fiona used static electricity to stick balloons all over her body. They were the long slender clown balloons, so we had about 10 future Weiner Dogs stuck to her fur. She'd let us do anything to her until we snapped the pic and gave her the release command. If you could interpret big sad hound eyes, they would have said:

"Really? This is the new low we're sinking to now? I'm a trained lifeguard, but you've got me dressed up like a fuckin' clown?!?"

Piper's puppy dog eyes were pretty convincing, but if they didn't work, she'd break out the big guns. First, she'd start whimpering while looking back and forth between you and the door. If that didn't get you off your ass, she'd jump to and fro, basically shaming you for not taking an old dog out to pee. When you finally got out of the chair, instead of going to the door, she'd herd you over to the treat drawer. Getting Yaya out of the La-Z-Boy with her shifty eyes was half the battle. To seal the deal, she'd shift back to her sad eyes and lay 'em on thick. That lying little bitch could have won an Oscar.

She was always putting on an act. She looked like Eeyore with her head sunk low until someone said "Okay!" That was her cue to shake it off and freak out – the zoomies feeding off our feeble attempts to chase her down.

There was no catching her. Except one time, when Finn and Fio were five, they crossed the street for the first time on their own. Mel and I were still waking up so it was unsanctioned, but they had accidentally let Piper slip out the front door and were in hot pursuit. I couldn't believe that Piper let them catch her, but there she was on the leash, in their hands. At full speed, she could leap across a 14-foot flood ditch, but somehow a five-year-old with his pants falling off caught her. Seems totally plausible.

I still have to finish the song, but who knows, maybe I'll get to sing it for her one day.

> Momma was a Hound
> Daddy was a Heeler
> She's a good dog
> As long as you feed her

Goodbye Scooby. Say hi to Buster and Honey Bear. You won't see Bosley. Even if Saint Peter let that old rascal past the pearly gates, he would have escaped by now.

I love you Piper. May you forever run in a treeless field full of squirrels.

"Get 'em!"

## Alexa, turn this bloody book off!

Jan. 15, 2025 | 15 y, 10 mo

Me: "Alexis, turn the TV off."

Alexa [Thinking]: "…"

Melina: "She doesn't answer to that. It's not her name. It's …"

Me: "Alexa! … turn the fucking TV off!!!"

Alexa [Considering the request]: "…"

Me: "Alexa you're retarded!"

Finn: "You're retarded. Just press the button on the remote."

Melina: "She doesn't respond to rudeness."

Me: "Alexa."

Alexa [Thinking animation swirls]: "…"

Me [calmly]: "Please … turn the motherfucking TV off."

Alexa [Swirls and swirls and swirls]: "…"

Melina: "Alexa, turn the TV off."

Alexa: "Sure!"

[ TV turns off ]

Me: "Oh my god."

Melina: "And she doesn't like foul language either."

Me: "Fuck you Alexa!"

Alexa: "You're welcome."

The end.

# Thank you...

Willow, for your poorly hidden diaries
that first inspired me to write.

Amber, my north star, for staying up past the
wee lunar hours, poking holes in the narrative.

Mom, my angel, for letting me run wild
at Silver Lake until dinner time.

Dad, for teaching me to play
all the things: guitar, ping
pong, baseball, goofball.

Buzz the Beast, for the Nashville
ass-whoopin' that started it all.

Melina, the best editor love can
buy. I'll get the tea going.

Finn and Fiona, my fraternal youth.
Keep living a life worthy of writing down.

# About the author

Darby's greatest fear in life is dying. Somewhere close behind is the fear that he might be dumb, or worse – that someday he'll do something really stupid and die like an idiot. The two fears really dovetail nicely.

This book is mostly an elaborate scheme to prove he was here and to validate himself so that he can stop worrying about impressing people and start worrying about doing all the things his wife would like him to do. (It's a very long list. In fact, he should be doing his Darby-dos right now instead of writing this puff piece.)

Darby's kids are super adorable – blah blah blah – and they're always stealing the show, which he secretly resents but outwardly encourages, like the supportive adult he sometimes remembers to be.

At last, he's found a way to capture their essence, bottle it up in a book, and smash it lovingly over your heads, along with a bunch of strange ideas you didn't sign up for when you read the title, which should have been:

**Eternal Goof**
*Weird Little Weirds and Other Weirdness*

The publisher wouldn't go for it.

Anyway, now that everything's out in the open, we can all relax and be real. Tell me your dreams. You want to start a band? I've always wanted to stand on a dark stage under hot lights and yell:

**"Thank you, Nashville! Y'all were a lot of fun. We're The Shit! Goodnight!"**

## A little Darb'll do ya

Content | Publishing | Performance: darbyjones+1@gmail.com
Writing: substack.com/@TheDarbyJones
Links: linktr.ee/TheDarbyJones
Music licensing: SoundCloud.com/JukeStone